Traveling
with God

Traveling with God

Joseph Murphy
Ph.D., D.D.

MEDIA

Published 2019 by Gildan Media LLC
aka G&D Media
www.GandDmedia.com

Design by Meghan Day Healey of Story Horse, LLC

Library of Congress Cataloging-in-Publication Data is available upon request

ISBN: 978-1-7225-0144-0

10   9   8   7   6   5   4   3   2   1

Contents

Introduction

This book is based on a spiritual travelogue or lecture tour around the world. This was due to a deep inner spiritual desire over a long period of time.

I left Los Angeles the latter part of April via the Polar Route for Europe.

We must learn to listen to the murmurings and the whisperings of our heart strings which guide us on to action. I was not on the lecture trip very long before I became aware of the reasons why I undertook the journey. You will learn my many reasons as you read the pages of this book. I am sure it will prove most interesting and revealing to you.

Traveling this Polar Route is inspiring. I shall never forget the experience as I looked out through the window of the plane and saw the dancing lights, the variegated colors. It seemed as if the whole sky above us were engulfed in a blaze of glory. This vast panorama of Northern Lights floods the Heavens with great flames that shoot upward, amazingly beautiful, awesomely unforgettable, reminding you that God is indescribable beauty.

A little girl said to her mother, "Mommy, look at God dancing in the skies." These Heavenly lights reminded me of the quotation in the Bible wherein it says, "This is the light that lighteth every man that cometh into the world." John 1:9.

As a boy, I used to watch the Northern Lights, but never have I seen such a display of God's handiwork as I saw through the windows of the plane as it neared the Arctic Circle. I could not help but think that God was all beauty, and absolute bliss and harmony; moreover to witness the Dance of God in the sky you are compelled to think of order, rhythm, beauty, and proportion.

The plane made a stop in Greenland for a few hours. It's simply marvelous to see how gracefully the pilot lands on that bleak, icy island. Immediately on landing we were taken to a little mountain cabin for coffee. There I met a man who said to me, "I used to listen to you in Los Angeles. Will you go and see my brother in Copenhagen?"

I said, "Yes."

He added, "I knew you were coming. I saw you in a dream and I knew also you could explain matters to my brother and straighten things out between us."

I asked him why he thought his brother would listen to me. He said that his brother reads all my books and is a great lover of *Magic of Faith*.

Upon landing in Copenhagen, I went to see this man. I explained my mission regarding his brother and I found that he had had an intense hatred toward his relative in Greenland over an imaginary wrong and had refused to write or answer his brother's letters.

He had a very stiff neck which oftentimes is due to resentment or ill will. We prayed together and he joined with me in radiating Love, Peace and Goodwill to his brother. I wrote down a simple prayer for him: "Divine love, Divine peace, and Divine harmony operate between my brother and myself at all times." Constant repetition of this prayer will help one solve any kind of misunderstanding. Prayer is a habit, and frequent occupancy of the mind with this prayer will recondition the mind to harmony, peace, and goodwill, resulting in the dissolution of the problem.

After our prayer together, he sat down and wrote a letter to his brother—it was beautiful and really would touch the heart-strings of any person. I began to think about his brother in Greenland who had a dream and saw me landing and entering the little cabin for coffee; which was provided some distance away from the landing-field. I felt very humble and began to marvel at the wonder of it all. "There are more things in Heaven and on earth than are dreamt of in our philosophy." Man does not always know the causes of his actions. There are times when a higher intelligence, you can call it the Fourth Dimensional Self, acts upon the mind of an individual causing him to be a messenger who fulfills the dream or desire of another. He may think he is doing it of his own volition, whereas actually the Higher Self or Infinite Intelligence within him compels him to act.

People in Denmark are very hospitable. A young man drove me into the country to a home with a thatched roof and several flower pots on the window sill. The hostess, on learning who I was, took the Bible from the library and asked me to write a special prayer for protection as she was going on a journey to Turkey by plane, and having never flown before, she was afraid. This is what I wrote: "The airplane is God's perfect idea and it moves from point to point freely, joyously, and lovingly. Divine love surrounds it, enfolds it. The Light of God envelops me at all times. God is the pilot of this plane, and all its parts are functioning perfectly. God and His presence fills my mind and heart, and I rest secure in His everlasting arms."

I have never seen anyone so happy and radiant as when she read this prayer. She exclaimed, "Oh, I am so happy; I never knew how to pray before!" In the twinkling of an eye she saw the Truth—that she was as safe traveling by air, as walking out into her own garden. The highways and byways of the sky were made by God, and God dwells everywhere.

Before giving a series of lectures and a special class in London, I went to Oslo, Norway's capital. On the plane I met a most interesting man who asked me, "Won't you speak for us in Oslo?" I did. All of them understood English perfectly. He had no particular religious belief, but said he belonged to a secret order. He got a group of his friends together and we discussed miracles of the subconscious mind together from 7:00 p.m. to 2:00 a.m. the next morning. This business executive, who has large interests in London, said, "I never knew such a teaching as this existed, but everything you've said to me on the plane and in our club, I have always believed." This goes to show you again that man instinctively knows the truth about himself when he hears it and has an open mind.

I found that Norway had cast a spell of enchantment around me. The scenic grandeur, its fascinating cities and interesting folkways captivated me. The mirrored beauty of the snow-clad peaks and sparkling glaciers reminded me that God truly is The One, The Beautiful and The Good.

In London I gave a series of lectures in Caxton Hall and also special classes in the afternoon under the auspices of the London Truth Forum which I founded in 1951 during a lecture tour in England. This wonderful group has expanded considerably and is now the largest Truth Forum in Europe. Its leader is Dr. E. Fleet, who is doing marvelous work in the propagation of the truth. It is most interesting to see the number of the nobility and aristocracy in England who are interested in this inner teaching of the Bible, which is simply a science of life. When I told these wonderful people that I was on a world lecture tour, they wrote letters to their friends in the various countries and gave me letters of introduction to many of the most influential people in some of the cities I was to visit. The usual statement rendered by members of the London audience was, "Oh, I want my sister in New Zealand," or "my brother in Australia," or "my friend in South Africa to hear you!"

Before I left London, Dr. Fleet arranged a dinner at one of the exclusive restaurants on the Strand where were gathered the most advanced students of London. In this informal gathering I heard the most fascinating personal accounts of the miracles of prayer which will live in my memory forever. To hear these wonderful people tell how prayer works won-ders, causes the Bell of God to ring in your heart.

From London I went to Ireland to speak at a place called Kilronan, Cloghron County, Dublin. Here are two wonderful people, Mr. and Mrs. George Dawson. They have spiritual gatherings at their beautiful home in the suburbs of Dublin. It really is a beautiful set-ting for a spiritual gathering and reminds you of the 23rd Psalm where it speaks of green pastures and still waters. I enjoyed the spiritual camaraderie here and I know that the labor of Love of Mr. and Mrs. Dawson prospers beyond their wildest dreams.

In the Shelbourne Hotel, in Dublin, I chatted with many men who asked about the New Thought teach-ing in America—what was it? They said that many of their relatives were returning to Ireland with all sorts of new ideas about religion. I found their conversation most refreshing and revealing.

One of my most ardent followers in Ireland is a relative of mine, a young man in Cork City who has made a deep study of all my writings, particularly *The Miracles of Your Mind, The Magic of Faith, Love Is Freedom* and other books and is now teaching the contents to small groups in the city of Cork and sur-rounding towns. He is doing it quietly and is gaining many adherents.

From here I went to Paris, France, where I spoke for a Unity Center, conducted by that famous, outstanding teacher, Dr. Mary Sterling. She is doing marvelous work in the propagation of Truth among the French people and is an outstanding authority on the French language. She is an English woman who speaks French without any trace of accent, and the French people take it for granted that she was born and educated in France. She has translated *Magic of Faith* and *The Miracles of Your Mind*, two of my very popular books, into French. They have been published in Paris by a well-known firm and are now finding their way into all French-speaking countries throughout the world.

From here I shall take my readers to Lourdes. The rest of this book was written en route between lectures and in various cities and countries visited.

1

My Visit to Lourdes

H ere, the blind see, the dumb speak, the deaf hear, the lame walk, the wounded and the lepers are healed." This is what a Frenchman said to me as I entered the Grotto during my recent visit to this Healing Shrine. I have visited many of the Healing Shrines in Europe and the Orient from time to time. This time, however, I did the unusual. I mingled with the pilgrims, bathed in the waters and talked to many patients, some of whom appeared to be hopeless cases. I visited the hospital where the people were cared for, talked to doctors and nurses, and to many others. An English doctor said, "Come and see my sister. We are not Catholics, but we came here to bathe in the waters." I talked with her. She had a remarkable healing. Her brother said it was cancer in the last stages. I asked him to what did he attribute the healing and his reply was, "The atmosphere of the place, plus faith."

I talked with many people from all parts of the world who were drinking the water. Many claimed relatives had been healed, and that they had been benefited by the water. I watched for hours. Hundreds of people were wheeled from the waters after immersion. There was a strange light in the eyes of some. In one instance, I wheeled a person and conversed with her. She said, "I know I am cured." I asked, "How do you know?" I wanted to hear her response. She replied, "It's an inner feeling which I can't describe. I know I shall walk tonight." She spoke perfect English and was from the northern part of France. She did walk that night, and I chatted with her for a long time. She said her healing was due to the fact that she invoked "Our Lady".

Why do these healings occur? The percentage is small; nevertheless, doctors, scientists, and others admit the healings. The question arises—why? We must admit that healings have taken place in all shrines throughout the world for countless generations. People have been healed at the Buddhistic shrines, and at the Shinto shrines of Japan, as well as at the shrines of Aesculapius. These people do not know anything about the Virgin Mary, or Jesus, or Moses; they are not interested; yet they have healings. The answer to all this is the simple truth that all healings are due to the Law of Belief.

There is only one Healing Presence—the Presence of God in man, and only one process of healing which is called Faith. There are, of course, many techniques and processes of healing, but actually there is no other healing power but that of the Living Intelligence within man which created him. It knows all the structures, processes, and functions of his entire body, and it can heal and restore any organ. Paracelus, 600 BC, said "Whether the object of your faith be true or false, you will get the same results." In other words, what he is saying is that all healings are due to belief. What is belief? To believe something is to mentally accept something as true.

Many of those patients I spoke to at Lourdes came from great distances full of faith and expecting that they would be healed. Their imagination was fired by the wonderful reports of healings and the prayers of the multitude plus the music which cast a sort of spell over them. All this tends to impregnate the subconscious mind with the idea of health or the expectation of a miracle.

The subconscious mind responds according to the belief of the person, and restores the organ to its Divine pattern. The Bible says "Whosoever shall say unto this mountain, Be thou removed, and be thou cast unto the sea; and shall not doubt in his heart, but shall believe that those things which he saith shall come to pass; he shall have whatsoever he saith." MARK 12:23. All things are possible to him that believeth.

In Ireland some years ago I saw a man practicing the laying on of hands. He said to me, "The great doctors who have gone on administer healings through me." He believed this himself. He had one striking cure in a case of paralysis. The trembling stopped and the man cried out, "I'm healed! I'm healed!" The operator believed that some great healer now living in the next dimension worked through him and that healing power flowed through his fingers.

The reader must see one simple explanation in all this—one healing power responding to man's belief. The ancient Greeks said, "The doctor dresses the wound and God heals it." The doctors say to you today, "Keep the wound clean and nature will heal it." Nature is the Infinite Healing Intelligence within you which made you and which has the Divine matrix or pattern for every cell of your body. It also knows exactly how to create new cells and new organs.

The mountain that is to be removed, of which the Bible speaks, is the obstacle, the impediment, the ailment, or the problem. When you pray, believing, the problem vanishes and disappears like ships at the bottom of the sea which are no longer seen. All you have to do, the Bible says, is believe in your heart (your sub-conscious mind) that what you say is true. Nothing else is required, only *believe*. "Jesus said unto him, If thou canst believe, all things are possible to him that believeth." MARK 9:23.

Could anything be plainer or simpler than that quotation of Jesus given over 2000 years ago? You don't have to believe in shrines, waters, springs, bones of Saints, or any thing, or any person—just have *Belief* itself. *Belief* is the law or cause of all healings in Lourdes, Shinto shrines, Buddhist shrines, or any other healing shrines. Belief causes this healing power of God within you to respond and manifest itself in your world. This spiritual power is positively and definitely the only healing power in the world. There is but one Power and one Presence. "Hear, O, Israel: The Lord our God is one Lord." DEUTERONOMY 6:4.

The Lord is the spiritual power which is one and indivisible. All men, doctors, churches, metaphysicians, psychiatrists, and psychoanalysts are using the one power. All doctors, whether they are osteopaths, chiropractors, allopathic physicians, or practitioners of homeopathy, are tapping the one universal healing power through the Law of Belief.

Look at your world now. By *your world* I mean your health, wealth, environment and circumstances. This power is distributed in all phases of your life according to the level of your belief. It is not the water or the kissing of the rock in the Grotto at Lourdes that heals; neither is it invoking the Virgin Mary to intercede for you or act as a mediator; rather, the result or healing you experience is due to belief in the mind. It is never the thing believed in or the person believed in; it is always mental acceptance or belief in your own mind that brings the response to your prayers. We do not criticize any person who seeks any form of healing; neither do we find fault with any religious group. All these groups and organizations are operating at the level of their belief; any church, organization, or healing method that alleviates the distress or suffering of mankind is, of course, good.

Every religion in the world is some form of belief, and they all worship the one God. We should rejoice to see the fundamental unity behind all religions. Divine Science and Psychology represent a true knowledge of God and how He works. It is true that no one can possibly know all about God, for God is Infinite; the finite mind can never fully encompass the Infinite. Nevertheless, we can discover certain functions of our conscious and subconscious mind. We can definitely determine how they work to a great extent. We can learn the power of our own thoughts and how this Infinite wisdom responds to our thought. We find that there is an answer to every problem within.

When we fill our minds with Love, Peace, Harmony, Goodwill and the Truth of God, our body and environment magically melt into the image and likeness of our habitual thinking.

We discover, as we change our thought and feelings, that we change our destiny. We learn by experience and application that thoughts are things. Man is what he thinks all day long. You can now, this very moment, wherever you are commune with this God-Power within through the medium of your own thought; the Presence and Power will respond according to the nature of your thought. You do not need any wafer or wine to experience a spiritual communion with the God-self. Inspiration can come to you as you read this book now. Still the wheels of your mind, relax, let go, say quietly and lovingly, "The God Presence within me flows through my intellect now as inspiration and guidance. I am inspired from On High and the Light of God illumines my intellect." Do this for about five minutes or so; you will experience a flow of energy and vitality coursing through your veins. Moreover, the Divine Wisdom will flood your mind, and God's ideas will begin to flow into your conscious awareness revealing to you everything you need to know, and showing you the way you should go. Actually, when you begin to awaken to the powers within you, you come to the definite conclusion that you need no external prop of any kind to make contact with the Almighty Power which doeth all things. You find you need no ritual, ceremony, liturgy, talismans, amulets, beads, candles, creeds, special rites, or forms of any kind. You come to the simple conclusion that good and evil are simply the movements of your own mind, and that your outer world forever corresponds with the inner pattern of your own mind.

Jesus said, "According to your faith be it unto you." You have heard the expression over and over again, "Faith moves mountains." "Thy faith hath made thee whole." Faith is a mental attitude, a way of thinking. It is like the attitude that when you deposit an apple seed in the ground, you will get an apple tree. You have faith that the sun will rise tomorrow morning. You have faith that you can drive your car, walk to business, do your work, or handle your profession successfully. You have faith that when you dial the right number, you will receive the answer. You may dial incorrectly for twenty years, but once you dial correctly you will receive the answer.

The farmer has faith in the laws of agriculture and waits with confidence for harvest time. The scientist working in his laboratory has faith in the possibility of the execution of the idea. All that the scientists or inventors have are invisible ideas in their minds. The scientist positively has faith that the wisdom which gave him the idea will also reveal to him everything he needs to know for its objective manifestation; so he keeps on experimenting, full of faith and perseverance, knowing that the way will be revealed. All great scientists, physicists and inventors are men of faith. They are dealing with the Invisible and Intangible, and they know and believe in their hearts that the invisible will be made visible. You could call faith "going in one direction only," knowing no opposition, because you believe in One Spiritual Power which knows no opposites and it has nothing to challenge it. To lack faith is to go in many directions, believing in two powers or having a divided mind. When you have faith, therefore, you identify yourself mentally with your ideal or goal, knowing in your heart or having a subjective feeling, that the Infinite Intelligence which gave you the idea will give it form and objectify it on the screen of visibility.

I was just asked, a few hours ago, in Paris where I am now lecturing at the Unity Centre, why it was that a person who was in a coma and unconscious, and who could not pray, was healed instantaneously when his brother went to the Grotto, lit a candle, and prayed for him at Lourdes. The answer is simple. There is only one mind; time and space are unknown in mind. Mind is one and indivisible. His brother was at the state of consciousness where he believed in forms, ceremonies, and external objects. By believing that his brother would be healed as he prayed to the Virgin to intercede, and by complying with certain forms and ceremonies, the response of the Spiritual Power acted according to his belief. It was not because of what he did or where he was. His belief was perfect health for his brother. This idea of perfection was immediately resurrected in the mind of his brother and the healing followed. It says in MARK 11:24, "What things soever ye desire, when ye pray, believe that ye receive them and ye shall have them." This passage says, "*You shall have them,*" indicating the automatic response of the law or action and reaction. The action was mentally accepting the idea of health and love. The reaction was the mental response or the answered prayer. All our experiences, conditions, events, and actions are merely the external manifestation of our habitual thinking.

I was asked after one of my lectures in Paris, "Is it true that the Bureau De Constatations, composed of distinguished physicians, acknowledged a percentage of remarkable healings taking place at Lourdes?" I replied that they admit remarkable healings; however, their explanations of those cures or healings vary.

Here is a question frequently propounded in Lourdes: "Why is it that the water which is obviously polluted with all kinds of virulent organisms and rarely renewed does not contaminate people?" I will answer this question by saying that it is again done unto us as we believe. The Law of Life is *belief*.

I went into the Piscines (baths) as they are called. I immersed myself in the bath. Many men, covered with all kinds of sores and loathsome diseases bathed in the same water. All were immersed in the same water. I was not the least bit afraid of contamination or infection. The attendant gets a sponge and sprays the water into your eyes and ears and prays as he does it. He chants a prayer to what he calls the Blessed Virgin and asks you to kiss the crucifix. He is sincere and quite religious and tells you in English that your healing will follow. I wanted to see first-hand what they did and what the reaction was of the people who were immersed. I found a simple blind faith, not based on understanding, but just a blind belief that something would happen. I do not recommend that you enter the water and bathe in it if you are afraid of germs and infection. That would be very foolish. If you have no fear, nothing, of course, will happen to you.

A physician said to me that according to microbial analysis the water contained a great many noxious germs. However, he added, the water is strongly antibiotic. That is to say, it destroys the virulence of the most noxious germs. Physicists have examined the water for radio-active power, and chemists for special minerals, but all to no avail. Others say results are due to penicillin. However, I am informed, exhaustive analysis by scientists produced no such evidence. Tuberculosis and cancer have been cured at Lourdes, but penicillin has not been used for such diseases. The question naturally continuously arises, "Why do not people get infected by this naturally polluted water?" It is due to belief. When you see a great mass of people praying and believing that the water is sacred and has healing powers, the belief of the multitude or of the individual is sufficient; and again according to their belief is it done unto them. "As thou hast believed, so be it done unto thee." The power is not in the water. The power and the result are in their belief.

People ask me if an unbeliever or a person who ridicules the entire procedure at Lourdes can be helped or healed. It is quite possible and has happened. I have been told of many such instances by people in the village of Lourdes. Incidentally, they are most friendly and speak English very well. The people in Lourdes are wonderful—very kind, courteous and most hospitable.

You are now asking, "How can an unbeliever be helped when it is done unto you as you believe." Through the years I have heard frequently that men and women come to scoff at metaphysical meetings and many went away healed. There is hardly a week passes by at the Wilshire Ebell Theatre that someone does not write and say, "I came to a meeting out of curiosity. I had migraine headaches regularly. I don't have them any more." or "I'm a Protestant, Lutheran, Jew, or Catholic and I came to your class highly skeptical but I had a marvelous healing." The reason is due to the prayers of others.

The Book of James says, "The prayer of faith shall save the sick, and the Lord shall raise them up." When you find the entire congregation joining together every Sunday at the Wilshire Ebell Theatre, praying that all those who are present be instantaneously healed, made whole and perfect, the exalted, spiritual atmosphere, or mood may well penetrate and melt the icy heart of someone, causing the Love of God to well up in the individual, resulting in a healing. There is no doubt that the spiritual atmosphere created at the theatre every Sunday morning where I speak in Los Angeles impinges itself on the receptive minds of people, resulting in answered prayer. An Infinite Healing Presence steals over that wonderful audience. I believe definitely it is the consciousness of Love that heals. The same is, of course, true at any shrine.

Here in Lourdes you find large bodies of people praying hourly for all the sick people in their own way, believing and expecting great things to happen. According to the law of belief, a person may be helped even though he is a so-called atheist, agnostic, or unbeliever. The belief of the multitude may heal him. Absent treatment or praying scientifically for a person who is not physically present has been practiced from time immemorial.

For example, a woman comes to a practitioner and says, "My husband is an alcoholic and does not believe in Divine healing or treatment." The practitioner begins to know and claim God's peace, and God's harmony floods his mind and heart, and his food and drink are God's ideas. Thus as the woman continues faithfully in knowing this truth about him even though he knows nothing about prayer, the treatment will become effective, and he will be freed from his destructive habit. As the practitioner frequently engages her mind with the idea of his freedom and peace of mind, results follow. It is the frequency, the habitual occupancy of the mind with the idea of his freedom and peace of mind that insures success. As the practitioner continues to pray for him, she reaches a conviction and a complete healing follows. The healing is the practitioner's belief in the patient's freedom. Healing begins first in the mind of the practitioner. There being only one mind, the alcoholic feels the conviction of the person praying, and it is made manifest. This is the basis of absent treatment.

In reality, there is no absent prayer or treatment for there is no absence in the One Presence. There is only One Mind. The other person is rooted in you, based upon your belief. Change your belief about the other person and results follow.

A Roman Catholic from San Francisco told me all his troubles in the hotel at Lourdes. I listened attentively. I never said anything to him, but that night in my meditation I imagined he told me what I wanted to hear. For ten or fifteen minutes prior to sleep I imagined he was in front of me, telling me about his wonderful answer to prayer. I heard it over and over again, finally going to sleep in the assurance that it was so. In the morning at breakfast, he told me more or less the same thing as I imagined him telling me. He had received a cable from America which solved his problem. This is the meaning of, "He calleth those things which be not as though they were." ROMANS 4:17.

People in Lourdes said to me, "I kissed the rock where the Virgin appeared and the soreness on my lips and face disappeared." By now you know there is no power in a piece of stone or rock, but the multitude may proclaim, pray, chant and sing that the rock is holy and all those touching it will be healed. Again we come back to the same principle. It is the belief that does the healing, not the rock. People transfer the power that is within themselves to rocks, stones, waters, fountains, etc., and all the while the God Presence within silently waits for man, saying "Come unto me, all ye that labour and are heavy laden, and I will give you rest." MATTHEW 11:28.

I had more invitations to private homes in India and Japan than it was possible to accept. I visited several, however, for dinner and was shown their altars to Buddha and also their Shinto Shrines. There was a beautiful spiritual atmosphere in these rooms dedicated to prayer and no one could help admiring their deep sincerity and devotion. One Japanese gentleman said, "This is the room where I pray for my ancestors just as though they were alive." His wife prepared breakfast for Buddha every morning. She told me, in faultless English, of her remarkable healing at one of the shrines. The same universal principle responds to all men according to their belief.

I visited the world famous shrine called Diabutsu in Japan. A gigantic Divinity of bronze is seated with folded hands and head inclined in an attitude of profound contemplative ecstasy. It is forty-two feet in height and is called the great Buddha. Here I saw young and old making offerings at its feet. Money, fruit, rice, and oranges are offered. Candles are lit, incense is burned, and prayers of petition given.

The guide explained the chant of a young girl as she murmured a prayer, bowed low and placed two oranges as an offering. She also lit a candle. He said she was thanking Buddha for restoring her voice. Again we come to the same fundamental truth behind all religions which are based on some belief about God and are, of course, all psychologically true. She had the simple faith that Buddha would give her back her singing voice if she followed a certain ritual, fasted perhaps, and made certain offerings. All this helped to kindle faith and expectancy, resulting in a conditioning of her mind to the point of belief, and her subconscious mind responded according to her belief. What the adherents of Buddha fail to see is that all parts of the great statue represent truths of God and that the figure itself is purely symbolic, reminding man of the God presence within him. For example, from the forehead protrudes a jewel from which light flows, reminding one of the truth in our own Scriptures. "I am the light of the world." JOHN 9:5. Your own IAMNESS or life principle is the Light or Infinite Intelligence present in all men everywhere.

It is not the belief in the water, the rock, or the shrine; but belief in the mind that brings results. The essence of the law of belief is given beautifully in the Bible, "For verily I say unto you, That whosoever shall say unto this mountain, Be thou removed, and be thou cast into the sea; and shall not doubt in his heart, but shall believe that those things which he saith shall come to pass; he shall have whatsoever he saith." MARK 11:23.

2

"Lord Teach Us To Pray"

Luke 11:1

I am writing a part of this chapter in South Africa. I flew on one of those magnificent, stately clippers from Rome to Cairo. Here in Egypt you subjectively feel the mood of mystery and romance about the illimitable treasures of this country, which is called the cradle of civilization. Here you meet archeologists, Egyptologists, writers, clergymen, adventurers, poets, artists, dreamers, and scholars. Somehow Egypt casts an enchanting spell over all of them, and they are held spellbound in the presence of the great pyramids and the Sphinx. The magnificent shrines and temples of the Pharaohs hold you enthralled.

Many of the guides are thoroughly versed in ancient, medieval and Egyptian history. One guide spoke eight languages fluently. He said to me that all languages were within his subconscious mind and that he had not had much trouble learning all the languages because he would constantly affirm morning, noon and night: "These languages are within me and I speak them fluently." He said he amazed his teachers by his rapid studies. Here you are given a lesson on the interaction of the conscious and subconscious mind. He was en-rapport with the subconscious mind. You know that when you tell your subconscious mind at night, "I want to wake up at 6:00 a.m.," and it awakens you. The principle behind it is this: You thought about 6:00 o'clock consciously prior to sleep. If you had not done so, it would not have awakened you. So this young man applied himself to the study of languages by consciously telling his deeper mind, "I speak these languages fluently and I have a perfect memory of all that I read and hear." There was a communion and cooperation between these two levels and the real function was in operation. Jesus said, "My Father worketh hitherto, and I work." John 5:17.

Journeying on to South Africa for the purpose of speaking in Capetown, Johannesburg and West Africa, we circled the world's greatest waterfall, Victoria, fully twice as high and as wide as Niagara. This is where Stanley met Livingston, besides Zulus, Pigmies, and Watussi giants. Watching the falls you are held spellbound, and the words of the Psalmist begin to steal gently over the arid areas of the mind, refreshing, soothing and restoring your soul. "Though the waters thereof roar and be troubled, though the mountains shake with the swelling thereof. Selah. There is a river, the streams whereof shall make glad the city of God, the holy place of the tabernacles of the most High. God is in the midst of her; she shall not be moved: God shall help her, and that right early." PSALMS 46:3, 6.

Jesus said in JOHN 4:14: "But whosoever drinketh of the water that I shall give him shall never thirst; but the water that I shall give him shall be in him a well of water springing up into everlasting life." All the passages in the Bible referring to water are intended to remind us that God in us is a Living Spirit and this Spirit is the water of our spiritual life. We can't live without water. It is in all things animate and so-called inanimate. To view this waterfall is to be reminded of the waters of life or spiritual refreshment.

After gazing on the beauty of Victoria Falls, a fellow-passenger said to me that he seemed to be in a sort of trance and suddenly an answer to a most perplexing problem came into his mind—this is what the inner water is. An answer welled up within him giving him peace and confidence. He came to that inner place within himself where the waters of life flow freely. The subjective wisdom always rises to the surface mind when it is stilled and serene. This is the

River of Peace which flows through your conscious mind and its streams make glad the City of God. The City of God is your own mind, at peace. All the people, namely thoughts, ideas, feelings and beliefs are now bathed by the internal river of peace. Go within yourself now; that is where the water of life is.

This man was terribly worried, confused, and perplexed and as his mind was stilled through contemplation of nature's beauty, a light broke into his mind and he saw clearly what to do. "Ho, every one that thirsteth, come ye to the waters, and he that hath no money; come ye, buy and eat; yea, come, buy wine and milk without money and without price." Isaiah 55:1.

Arriving at Johannesburg, I found the local Truth Center closed down as the teacher was away on a lecture tour. I interviewed a number of people there at the request of Dr. Brunt of Capetown. I was asking for guidance for the opportunity to lecture there. One of the people who interviewed me said, "My husband would love to have you lecture," and he called up all his friends and acquaintances in Truth and we had a lovely time in Johannesburg. The answer comes, sometimes, in strange ways. "For as the heavens are higher than the earth, so are my ways higher than your ways, and my thoughts than your thoughts." Isaiah 55:9.

I desired to visit the famous Kruger Park while in Johannesburg and the hotel management said, "You are too late—there will be no tour until next Monday." My time was running short there and I said to my deep self, "Infinite Spirit opens up the way where man says there is no way." Chatting with a man from Kimberley at breakfast, he told me of his problem, and I gave him a copy of *The Miracles of the Mind* and told him what to do. The next morning he said he never knew such simple methods of prayer existed and that he had no longer a problem. Then he told me that he and his chauffeur were going to Kruger Park, the great preserve, passing through tribal villages of Zulus, photographing everything from zebras and rhinos to giraffes out on the endless veld. He said, "We are going to see lions, baboons and elephants, birds that cry 'go away' and all kinds of animals for which I have no name." Then he suddenly said, "We would deem it an honor to have you join us. You are my guest." I couldn't say "no". This was the answer to my prayer. "For as the heavens are higher than the earth so are my ways higher than your ways." ISAIAH 55:9.

"Our Father which art in heaven,
Hallowed be thy name.
Thy kingdom come.
Thy will be done in earth, as it is in heaven.
Give us this day our daily bread.

And forgive us our debts, as we forgive our debtors.
And lead us not into temptation,
but deliver us from evil:
For thine is the kingdom, and the power,
and the glory, for ever.
Amen."
MATTHEW 6:9, 10, 11, 12, 13.

As we traveled, we discussed the meaning of the Lord's prayer. He had been asking many questions the previous night and I had promised to discuss this wonderful prayer. He said he had always looked upon it as a "must" prayer and that he said it every morning and also at night prior to retiring, but did not know whether it meant anything or not. Prayer is not vain repetition. Prayer, to be real and sincere, must be a movement of the heart and not of the lips. I told him I had recently spoken at Lourdes on the inner meaning of the Lord's Prayer and the following is the essence of my discussion with him and also at Lourdes.

When you say "Our Father" it means all of us have a common Father, that we are all brothers and sisters. All of us come from the one source. God is Life and all things come forth from the one Life principle. The two first words "Our Father" sum up the Lord's Prayer; it is the foundation upon which the whole prayer is based. In these two words are your enfranchisement, your happiness, and your peace of mind. Looking upon God as your Father reveals to you a source of power and strength for all your needs. The word "Father" denotes love, care protection, provider. Your human father watches over you, provides for you, labors for your welfare. He sees to it that you are provided with shelter, food, raiment, assurance and other constructive moods which help you grow physically, mentally and emotionally. In our early days our parents stand for God. However, behind the father and mother stands the eternal truth, "Every good gift and perfect gift is from above, and cometh down from the Father of lights, with whom is no variableness, neither shadow of turning." JAMES 1:17.

The word Father means also the Creator, the Creative Principle of Life. When you say "Our Father" you are talking about the Supreme Being, the Infinite Power, the Creative Principle from which all things flow. You know, if I look at you, I do not see the real man. I do not see your thoughts, feelings, hopes, joys, fears, vacuities, yearnings, aspirations, desires, plans, schemes, ideas, etc. All these are invisible. I do not see your mind, your spirit. You are really invisible. All I see is your form, the outline of your body. The invisible power in you is your Father—it is the creative power. It is impossible to know all there is about it. The finite mind can never fully comprehend the

Infinite, but one certainly can learn about those inner powers. We can learn the power of our thoughts and feeling, our actions and reactions, and there is much we can learn about the laws of our own being.

The Bible says, "It is the Father within which doeth the works." You lift the book—this is the power of your own awareness or consciousness; this is the Eternal Principle which never was born and never dies. Your consciousness is perpetual motion. It is eternal and divine. Push the chair aside. It is not your body doing that—it is the spirit within, the Creative Power. When you walk, talk, or lift the receiver—it is the Invisible Power in you acting in the body, telephone or type-writer as the case may be. The self-moving power is within you. The Unmoved Mover of all is within you. The body does nothing of itself. As you know, it has, as Quimby says, no initiative, no volition. It does not talk back to you. It responds to your thought. Our Father is the name given to this God power or Presence within us to remind us it is a beneficent, kindly power. It is the creative omnipresent power and Lord of all creation.

This invisible spiritual power is your Father. If you think of this power as cruel, tyrannical, and vengeful, then, of course, you experience the results of your own negative thinking. If you think God is punishing you, testing you, your own negative thought and imagery causes you to suffer accordingly.

Awaken now and look upon this Spiritual Power as a Loving Father who watches over you, cares for you, guides you and inspires you and this Spiritual Power will respond as a benediction and a blessing upon you. You will find yourself guided in all your ways and protected from negative experiences of all nature. You will also find true expression and prosperity by praying in this simple manner. Remember, as you turn to It, It turns to you, because Its nature is to respond according to the nature of your thought.

To know God is to look upon him as your friend, benefactor, guide and counsellor. The Bible, in the book of ISAIAH 9:6 says, "His name is Wonderful Counsellor, The Mighty God, The everlasting Father, The Prince of Peace." Here is the whole story. Enthrone that concept of God in your mind and live with it and your whole world will magically melt into the image and likeness of your habitual concept. By mentally dwelling on this concept of God you will experience the reaction as love, peace, inspiration and energy. You now look upon the power as a Father who loves, cares and sends good things into your life and watch your world change accordingly.

The word Heaven means the Invisible State. In the absolute state it means bliss, indescribable beauty, and boundless love. You are told the Kingdom of Heaven is within you which means Infinite Intelligence, Boundless Wisdom, Omnipotence, and all the qualities and attributes of God are within you. These powers are in your own unconscious depths waiting to be brought forth by prayer and meditation. The treasure house of Infinity is within the heavens of your own mind. Relatively speaking, you are in Heaven when your mind is at peace; i.e., when you are poised, serene, and calm.

"Our Father which art in Heaven" MATTHEW 6:9, means the Invisible Spiritual Power which is infinite, timeless, shapeless and ageless. The word "Heaven" means it is without face, form or figure. As Troward so eloquently points out, Infinity cannot be multiplied or divided. The Infinite must be one—a unity, and there cannot be two Infinites, as one, he says, would quarrel with the other and they would neutralize each other. We would have a chaos instead of a cosmos. Unity of the spirit is a mathematical necessity and there is no opposition to the one power. If there were some power to challenge the Infinite one, it would cease to be Omnipotent or Infinite.

You can now see what confusion and chaos reigns in the minds of people who believe in two opposing powers. Their minds are divided because they have two masters, which creates a conflict, and causes their power and strength to be split. Learn to go in one direction only by believing in the one true God, your everlasting Father.

Here in Johannesburg, where I am interviewing and lecturing, it is called South Africa's Golden City, a city of laughter, gaiety, money and also troubled hearts. I was informed here by the hotel manager that sixty years ago Johannesburg was only a mining camp, and seventy years ago there was a vast jungle where paved streets and skyscrapers now stand. Here you find the hustle and bustle of New York City. The land where Johannesburg stands was offered to a man for eight oxen, sixty years ago. The owner wanted twelve, so for four oxen, the buyer, Mr. Jennings, did not purchase the land which in sixty years has so much wealth it would make Midas and Croesus appear as beggars. Had he known how to pray he would have advanced his offer to twelve oxen which was the price asked. Obviously he did not ask for Guidance and right action in his business affairs. Underneath this great city are gold mines reaching ten thousand feet below the surface. You find a city beneath a city. Here the native workers from all parts of Africa work extracting and refining gold.

The manager of one of the compounds where the colored people live who work in the mines had charge of nine thousand employees. The tribes are kept in separate rooms and quarters as they have different tribal customs, languages and gods. Some of these tribes are very primitive and superstitious. The manager, a Scotchman, told me that when the witch doctor prays the death prayer against the natives, all the doctors they have can't help them, they die. In other words, the native kills himself through fear but he doesn't know the reason. The same prayer by the voodoo doctor has no effect on the white missionary as he laughs at the witch doctor's incantations, showing you again the power of belief. The enemies are in your own mind and nowhere else. No one has any power over you unless you give him power in your own mind. The Spirit within you is the only sovereign and supreme power. It is one and indivisible and always responds to your thought.

I met a woman here in Johannesburg, South Africa where I am writing this book and giving lectures. She has six children, one of whom is a man aged about forty-five. She taught all her children to look upon God as the Great Father who would always guide and watch over them, sustaining them in all their ways. The son who works in the gold mine here said he was told he couldn't live more than six months and he said to the good doctor, "Doctor, my Father couldn't or just wouldn't do that to me. I have three children. They need me and my Father loves me. He will heal me." The doctor thought he was joking but the man explained to him what he meant and he and the doctor became good friends. He had a healing and is now very strong and powerful and has a leading position in one of the gold mines here. This young man told me that there were times when the family couldn't see a way out of seemingly impossible situations, but his mother would have them all talk to the Father within, and because of His love for them he would respond, and the miracle always happened. This family leads a charmed life because they look on God as their "Father," kind, loving, understanding, and compassionate. A sister of this man had poliomyelitis and walks perfectly. I chatted with her and she said the same thing as her brother, "God, my Father, couldn't or would not want His daughter to be crippled. My Father wants me to be happy." I asked her how she prayed when she was a little girl and she said, "Every night I used to say, 'Loving Father, make your daughter whole, so she can sing and dance and be gay.' I was healed in two years."

"Hallowed be thy name." The word "Hallowed" means wholeness, purity, perfection. The Bible says it is "The Holy one who inhabiteth eternity, whose name is perfect." ISAIAH 57:15. This means, of course, that God is Infinite Perfection, Absolute Bliss, Indescribable Beauty, Boundless Wisdom, and Absolute Harmony. Wholeness also means Unity, a oneness. There cannot be another. The word Name means the nature and character of the thing named. If I call you

John Jones, it means not only your name, but your race, your social status, your wealth, your education, your family life and all things appertaining to you. It is your identity in the Universal Mind. "Hear, O Israel: the Lord, our God is one Lord." DEUTERONOMY 6:4.

You hallow the name when you recognize there is only one spiritual power which is omnipotent and supreme, exercising authority over your life. When your thought is constructive, harmonious, and sincere, this power responds as Mercy, as Love, as a Benediction, blessing and prospering you in all your ways.

You are hallowing the name of God when you mentally accept the fact that this power brings only goodness, truth and beauty into your life. It is forever responsive to your thought.

I just finished talking to a wonderful man from Kimberley. I told him I would refer to him in my new book. He was a soldier in the war and his leg was broken by gunfire. He knew nothing about The Healing Power within and said he was an atheist at that time. When the Army asked him his religion he said "Human Being." He was on crutches in an English hospital for a long time. He began to think, and he said to himself, "There is an Intelligence which made me, and it can heal my leg." He began to picture himself doing all the things he would do were he whole and perfect. Formerly he was an athlete. He lived the life of an athlete in his mind, having a picture of himself as he wanted to be. He participated in the mental motion, he dramatized it, felt it and made it real. He said he was unable to walk, but on the chair, he would feel himself riding a bicycle, climbing mountains or kicking a football. Furthermore, he began to claim he was strong and powerful. The amazing result of this was that in a few years he was pronounced the strongest man in South Africa for his size. His leg healed perfectly where the major bones were broken. He showed me his leg and there is only a scar there.

He hallowed the name of God by feeling himself whole and perfect, refusing to let his attention be distracted from his objective or goal. If he began to worry, fret, fuss and fume, he would not be hallowing the name. When he loved his ideal to the exclusion of everything else, he was really progressing and feeling the naturalness of the state sought.

The name is the nature or naturalness of the state prayed for. It is entering into a mood, feeling or mental atmosphere or actually living mentally with the state until complete mental absorption takes place.

In interviewing some people in Africa, I had a most interesting talk with a brilliant man from Europe. After the war he was one of those men without a country. He could not prove his identity. His home was destroyed and all his relatives and members of his family were killed. He wanted a passport. It was hopeless. He said he was refused many times. He said that in his own simple way he began to picture the Consul stamping his imaginary passport night after night. Subsequent to his prayer, people came into his experience who testified and swore to his origin and background and papers were issued. He said meeting them was the strangest experience in the world. God's ways are past finding out.

"Thy Kingdom come." The Kingdom of Heaven is at hand. If someone says, "Lo here, lo there, believe them not, for the Kingdom of Heaven is at hand." God is within you, the very life of you. God is the Life and that Life is your life now. God is the Life Principle. God never forsakes you nor leaves you. I do not look for God's Kingdom to come—it is here now, within me. It is omnipresent. Recognize now, One Spiritual Power present everywhere. Everything in the world is made inside and out of it. Infinite Wisdom is within you at this moment, waiting for you to call upon it.

In speaking and conversing with people in Kruger Park, the great national preserve, one man from Livingstone who attended a few of my public lectures in Capetown said he had been praying for guidance regarding a human relations problem when a friend sent him a circular about my lectures in Capetown, South Africa. He flew down and received his answer.

Moreover, while there, he was offered a most attractive, lucrative position which he accepted. This man must have asked five hundred questions in two days. He recognized that the Kingdom of God's infinite riches were within. He called upon It and It answered him. He was guided to his right place. He was doubly blessed.

Each person is a king in his own mind. You are master of your thought reactions. You can now order your thoughts around as you like, letting them give attention to whatever you choose to meditate on. Our emotion follows thought. You can tell your employees what to do and they obey you. You are a king, a monarch in your conceptive realm. You can refuse a passport to any foreign visitors to enter your kingdom, such as fear, doubt, worry, anxiety, criticisms, hatred, etc. You are a king and you order your subjects around and they must obey you, for you are an absolute monarch with power to kill, destroy and obliterate all enemies (negative thoughts) from your mental kingdom. You can do this with the fire of Divine Love or the right thought. You determine the mood or feeling you shall entertain. You can decide how you shall react to conditions, circumstances and environment. If unpleasant news comes to you by courier or messenger, if others criticize, condemn and vilify you, remember you are a king and no one can hurt or injure you unless you give permission through your mental consent. Refuse permission and do not allow any negative thought to disturb you. You should positively refuse to react negatively. Say, "I am a King, walking the King's Highway. I remain unmoved, undisturbed, as nothing affects me except my own thought and through my own mental consent. I give allegiance and loyalty only to God and His Truths." "Thou sayest that I am a King and for this end was I born."

You were born to express more and more of God here and now and to let your light so shine that men see your good works, thereby glorifying your Father which is in Heaven. You are not begging or beseeching for some kingdom to come for it is your Father's good pleasure to give you the kingdom. God's Kingdom is come when you really see to it that your mind is governed and controlled by Divine ideas which activate, heal, restore, and inspire the mind. Our mind is controlled by ideas. Quimby says, "Man moves as he is moved upon. Man acts as he is acted upon." Ideas control you and the ideas you live with in your mind cause you to act the way you do. You are a king and you shall decree a thing and it shall come to pass. Your mood, your feeling, your conviction is your command to the deeper mind which automatically responds to your inner feeling and belief. No one talks back to you because you are the sovereign exercising supreme authority over your household and all your servants who are your thoughts, ideas, feelings and emotions, faithfully carrying out your orders. You are a king, traveling the King's Highway, and you are always sending messengers before you, based on your habitual thinking. These messengers prepare the way for you. In ancient times and even to the present time, when kings traveled, couriers and messengers were sent forth to prepare everything and get everything in readiness for the King. A royal welcome was assured. Likewise, soldiers searched the route in the same manner as when a president goes on a trip. Secret service men go over the route and examine rail tracks and platforms, keeping a watchful eye at all times. No thieves or robbers or gangsters can come near the king as he travels because of all the precautions taken for his safety.

As you walk in the consciousness of God's Love and as you pray that Divine Love goes before you to make straight, joyous, happy and beautiful your way, and as you live with that assumption, you too will have wonderful experiences on your journey and meet wonderful people. Wherever you travel be sure to issue orders to your people (your thoughts and feelings) to prepare the way for you so you will be assured of a royal welcome wherever you go.

I am writing this chapter in Capetown, South Africa, a beautiful city. Here you feel quite at home among friendly English-speaking people. Their accent seems to be the same as that of the people in London. I said to several students of Dr. Hester Brunt who is the Director of the Science of Mind in this city, "Are you from England?" They said, "No, born here." But their parents were from England which indicates the mental and spiritual atmosphere of the home, conditions and influences the child, wherever he may be born.

Dr. Brunt and her able assistants showed me the interesting spots around Capetown, the magnificent garden drive and its proud heritage of Cecil Rhodes and the early Dutch. Capetown resembles Hollywood at night. There is a wonderful Science of Mind Center here, and Dr. Brunt told me many Americans who come to her Centre ask her where are the lions and tigers. They seem to think that all you have to do is go outside the town a few miles and you will see them. This, of course, is not true.

For the adventure of a lifetime, it would fascinate and enthrall you to go to Kruger National Park where I saw big game run wild and strange lions strop their backbones against the mud-guard of your car. I saw one man get out of his car and take a photograph of a black rhino, and when the rhino suddenly charged, the man had to run up a tree and remain there. We prayed for him in this manner, knowing that God's Love is in all his creatures, and as we radiated Love and Peace to the animal, it walked away and the man came down from the tree. He was an American who failed to observe the instructions of the guide.

Dr. Brunt and her daughter are doing marvelous work in the propagation of the Truth and their work is penetrating all parts of the Union.

I chatted with a man in the Grand Hotel in Capetown, South Africa who said to me, "When I travel, I travel like a king. God is a multimillionaire." I liked his attitude and asked him to elaborate and elucidate further and he did. He said, "When I left England by plane I said 'This plane is God's idea and all its parts are God's ideas and all the people are God's Beloved and God loves them and so do I. Peace, abundance, love, joy and inspiration attend me on the way.'"

He repeated those phrases frequently until, by a process of mental and spiritual osmosis, these ideas penetrated the depths of his subconscious mind. This man has had the most wonderful experiences, and though a complete stranger in Capetown, made very desirable contacts both business and financial. He met the girl of his dreams, and when I talked to him he was madly in love and had no appetite. Lovers lose their appetites, you know. He decreed that the messengers of peace, love, joy, and abundance would wait on him at all times. Behold, I send my messenger and he shall prepare the way. The next time you travel, be sure you are a King, living now in the Kingdom of God or all good. All the good you want is here now, waiting for you to claim it. "The works are finished." HEBREWS 4:3. "I am the beginning and the end, there is nothing to come that has not been and is." ECCLESIASTES 3:15.

Whatever you mentally feel and accept as true comes to pass. We actually give form and expression to that which already is. Actually, we create nothing. We do not create electricity. We display it or use it. We do not create peace. We manifest it by our mental attitude. Think for a moment of God's infinite ideas, there is only one Self Originator. Whatever you think of already is; otherwise, you couldn't think it.

Look at your piano. All tones are within it. All musical compositions are there. All you do is rearrange the notes and bring forth the melody which was there already. You can play a melody of love or a funeral dirge. You don't create the notes. The music and the tones were there from the foundation of time.

"Thy will be done on earth as it is in Heaven." A wonderful prayer. Realize that God's will is always being expressed through you at all times. Make a habit of affirming that God's will is being expressed in all departments of your life, making certain of course, that you know what you mean when you say, "God's will is done."

The will of God is the nature of God, and God's name or nature as you have learned in Isaiah 9:6. is called Wonderful, Mighty God, Everlasting Father, Counsellor and Prince of Peace. God is Boundless Love, Absolute Bliss, Indescribable Beauty, Infinite Intelligence, Absolute Harmony, Omnipotent, Supreme and Absolute Peace. There are no divisions or quarrels in the Absolute. God's will for you must therefore be something wonderful, magnificent, glorious and far surpassing your wildest dreams. God is Life and His will for you must be to express a greater measure of life, i.e., to lead a full and happy life. Life cannot wish death. That would be a contradiction of God's nature or God's will, for the will of God is always the nature of God, and God is infinitely good and perfect and the author only of perfect good. Pray aright in this way, "God's will is being made manifest in my life as perfect health, harmony, happiness, peace, joy, abundance, love and perfect Divine expression. It is wonderful."

If you meditate on the above prayer regularly, your present environment and circumstances will magically change and be transformed into the likeness of what you are contemplating.

The inner meaning of the Lord's prayer which I am writing about was given in essence to a group of English-speaking visitors and tourists at Lourdes during my visit there, and I am writing part of it while lecturing in South Africa, Australia, New Zealand, India and Japan.

Now, when you say God's will is operating in my life it has a magnificent and beautiful significance full of spiritual precious stones. When you say God's plan is made manifest in my life, that too has a new and wonderful meaning. God's plan is God's will and His plan can only be Beauty, Order, Symmetry, Love, Health, and all the good things of life. God's plan for you could only be to express more of Himself moving ever onward, upward and Godward. Jesus said, "As thou hast believed, so be it done unto thee."

I said to a British pilgrim to Lourdes who was staying with his boy in a hotel near mine, "What do you mean when you say 'If it is God's will, my boy will be healed'? Surely God's will for the boy must, by the very nature of God, be perfect health for the boy.'" "I am come that you might have life and have it more abundantly." John 10:10.

He seemed doubtful and puzzled. He seemed to think that God's will for the boy must be something unpleasant or evil. What a monstrous concept of God! When you say "if" it means you are full of doubt, fear and anxiety. There is no "if" in prayer. Cross it out! Never, never say "if it's God's will" or "if it's right for me." What isn't right for you? Do you have two God's or one? When you pray for right action, there is only right action. Surely, you are not thinking of wrong action. If you are thinking of wrong action you have two powers, God and a Devil. Begin to put the true God back on the throne of His Glory in your mind.

This man was one of the pilgrims who listened to my explanation of the Lord's prayer. He seemed deeply moved and touched by the presence of God within him. He said, with tears in his eyes, "I now know what God's will for my boy is and I am going to claim it, feel it and believe it until it becomes a part of my consciousness and when I reach a conviction in my mind, then my will or desire becomes God's will or the conviction that 'it is done'."

How simple the whole thing is, how beautiful! Why do we complicate these simple truths of God so that men fear God instead of loving His Holy Presence?

The few days I was in Lourdes saw a remarkable change in this boy. The boy began to say meaningfully and with a light in his eye, "God's will is made manifest in my mind and body, and God walks and talks in me."

I bade them goodby and I know in my heart that the Father and the boy will both have the ecstasy and the joy and the thrill of witnessing and experiencing God's Holy Will.

What a magnificent prayer. What superb spiritual strategy to say "God's will be done." "As thou hast believed, so be it done unto thee." MATTHEW 8:13. All it means is this: if you enthrone in your mind the definite idea that God's will is operating in all your affairs, this positive belief in your mind will govern your life and cause you to act and express yourself as you believe. Your dominant conviction dictates, governs and controls your entire life. It is a wonderful thing to know, as Quimby expressed it, that "man is belief expressed." When you know that the Light and Love of God are guiding and governing you in all your ways, you are automatically protected from making errors in judgment, unwise decisions and wasting your time and efforts along useless lines of endeavor.

In Dublin, after a lecture on *The Miracles of Your Mind,* one of my more popular sellers, a man asked me this question, "How do I know if God wants me to leave my position and open up my own business?" Such a question, of course, can be easily answered. The desire to go into business for himself is good and very good. It is Life seeking a higher expression through him. His desire for advancement and greater expression is good.

I told him not to sit around wondering whether God wanted him to be a butcher, baker or candlestick maker, but to do the obvious, common sense thing. He is here on this plane to express, to grow, expand and unfold. If his desire is good and hurts no one, that is the will of God for him. I added firmly that he should deal positively and lovingly with his desire, knowing in his heart his prayer for God's guidance would watch over him, governing and sustaining, providing all things necessary for the realization of his dreams.

This young man realized that his mission was to welcome his desire for growth, nourish the idea in his mind and accept the good, knowing that Infinite Intelligence was guiding him in all its ways. His thought, being wise, his action must be wise also, for wise action follows wise thought. Action and reaction are universal throughout nature. When his premise is right, the result must also be right. It is through desire we grow. Your desire is God's gift to you. It is God's promise of fulfillment. A seed is a promise of a harvest. God is speaking to you now through the murmurings and whisperings of your heartstrings, perhaps in the field of music, drama, voice, etc. Accept your desire as a living reality now and walk in the light that it is yours. Maintain your belief in the reality of your ideal or plan until it becomes manifest in your experience.

In Oslo, Norway, where I spoke to a group in a private home, one of the group, a distinguished linguist, said, "What steps should I take after I fully believe that my prayer is answered?" The answer to that is that he will be compelled to take whatever footsteps are necessary for the fulfillment of his desire.

The law of the subconscious is compulsion. Man's subconscious beliefs and assumptions dictate, control and govern all his conscious actions. You don't aid the Infinite One. Everything you seem to do automatically happens according to your belief. You may think you are doing something but all your steps are controlled by the Deeper Self. You have freedom in this sense; you have free will in the choice of the idea, desire, or concept you entertain. As you mentally accept the idea as a living reality now, it becomes manifest in your world. Everything you do or whatever happens takes place because of your belief. When you assume something to be true in your mind, the subjective wisdom directs your actions automatically. He said he fully understood.

A woman asked me in Caxton Hall, London, where I gave a series of special classes, "What club should I join to meet men? In my work there are no men, all girls. I live alone, belong to no organizations, don't dance, swim or golf and I never meet men. What objective steps should I take after praying for my ideal companion?" My answer was that there was noth- ing to do, only to pray believing, and as she filled her mind with the qualities she admired in a man, then the seed would be planted and grow. She planted the seed by quietly dwelling on the fact that Infinite Intelligence revealed to her now a man with whom she harmonized perfectly, that he was spiritual, loyal, faithful, etc. When she had appropriated these qualities by mentally eating of them, she would automatically attract the image and likeness of her inner mood, and that's exactly what happened. She was going to the postoffice with office mail when a man in a hurry knocked all the bundles from her arm. He apologized profusely and asked her to dinner. She brought him to my lectures and said, "We are engaged. Here is my answered prayer."

This question of what shall I do after believing in the reality of my desire is a delusion; the deepself brings it to pass in its own way, and whatever you do, whether you go to a dance, swim, or join a club has nothing to do with it. What you believe and accept in your mind causes you to take whatever footsteps are necessary and everything, as Ouspensky says, just "happens." The Bible says not my will be done, but Thine be done. You have learned what God's will is. It is Divine right action and all things good.

Enter into the joy of the answered prayer, and your will (wish, idea, desire) will become God's will or the consciousness of having or being what you long to be or possess. This is the consciousness of conviction which manifests itself in your world as a condition, experience or event.

"Thy will be done on earth as it is in Heaven" is a wonderful prayer as you now realize. Heaven means your own mind or mental atmosphere, and what you feel as true in the heavens of your own mind, you shall experience on earth or the objective plane (body, world, environment, circumstances).

Your will is your capacity to choose your goal, ideal or objective. Live with it mentally by loving it, nursing it, giving it your attention and whole-souled devotion. Finally it gels within you and your will has become God's will or the joy of the answered prayer. It is wonderful.

"Give us this day our daily bread." The bread spoken of represents not only every material thing you need in this world, such as food, raiment, clothing, expression, etc., but also the bread of the silence. We must eat of the bread of Heaven and our cry must be, "Lord evermore give us this bread." JOHN 6:34. You may eat of the choicest foods and be hungry in your heart for peace, joy, love, happiness and inspiration. Every day of your life, mentally eat of God's ideas of wisdom, truth and beauty. You eat of the bread of Heaven whenever you turn away from the world, sense-evidence and feast on the Truth that there is only one power operating through the thoughts, feelings and imagery of your own mind. Shakespeare says, "Man's inhumanity to man makes countless thousands mourn."

When you read the newspapers, listen to the radio and press reports, you read of suffering, war, crime, injustice, poverty, and lack of all kinds. Perhaps you may feel the strains and stresses of your business or profession. Maybe the vexations, arguments and difficulties of the day have unduly upset you. If so, begin now to eat regularly of the bread of Heaven. Go in to the secret place of your own mind where you will not suffer from distractions caused by sense perceptions of the outer world. Think of God and Heaven and commune with that inner peace. You are now eating of the blessed bread of Heaven. In this secret place where God dwells there is peace, light, nourishment, energy and power to feed your mind and soul, enabling you to overcome the stress and strain, giving you vitality and enthusiasm for tomorrow's or next week's work. Reject the false beliefs and the hypnosis of the world, and affirm in your own heart the supreme sovereignty of the spiritual power of the God-Self within you. You can overcome all things in your world with such faith and conviction.

Do not permit your mind to become paralyzed and hypnotized by the avalanche of sights and sounds presented by the five senses. Turn back to God and

His presence in you. Mentally dwell on His wholeness, perfection, power and wisdom until your mind is lifted up and exalted. As you do this your mind will be fascinated, engrossed and absorbed in the great truths you are feasting on. You are eating of your daily bread, and you will hunger no more, nor thirst any more, for God in His wisdom, becomes a lamp unto your feet and a light on your path.

"My Father giveth you the true bread from Heaven." JOHN 6:32. "I am the bread of life." JOHN 6:35. Here you are told plainly that I am (God) is the true bread, eat mentally of all things good, eat of your desire now, mentally appropriate it, feast on its reality until it becomes a part of you, and when your mind is filled with the feeling of being what you long to be, you have eaten of the idea or of your good.

God and good are synonymous. "I am that bread of life." JOHN 6:48. "The words that I speak unto you, they are spirit, and they are life" JOHN 6:63. Here Jesus states explicitly that his words are spirit and life and are not to be taken literally.

The Bible says "He took bread, and gave thanks, and brake it, and gave unto them saying, This is my body which is given for you: this do in remembrance of me." LUKE 22:19. Surely this is not to be taken literally. We have already seen that the language is mystical, allegorical and figurative. It is not actual bread but psychological food. The seed holds within it the body or form of the plant or tree; likewise the idea or desire you feast upon mentally has within it its own mathematics and mechanics. All you do is accept the idea and the subjective self clothes the idea and projects it onto the screen of visibility. To eat of your desire is to eat of the body of Christ, for Christ is the fulfilling of the law. Christ means your consciousness at peace or the consciousness of fullness or the inner conviction that your prayer is answered. Christ means the wisdom and power of God functioning in your mind.

When you are praying or feasting on the reality of your desire you are feasting on Christ. Likewise, as you dwell on the glory and the beauty of God, as you contemplate that which is elevating and dignifying, you are actually eating of the body of Christ for these states will take form and become embodied in your world.

The body and form is already contained in the idea meditated on. Share this bread of Heaven with others. It's the bread of love, goodwill, understanding and the spirit of forgiveness. Practice the prayer of "give us this day our daily bread" by listening from this moment to the voice of your Heavenly Father, and your father is God. You call no man on earth your Father; only God is your Father, and you are now under Divine orders to bring forth harmony, health and peace.

Eat the bread of Heaven and live life gloriously by enthroning Wisdom as your Father and Love for your Mother. This is the Father-Mother God. The issue from this Divine union is Health, Happiness, Peace, Goodwill, Inspiration, Guidance and Illumination. "Lord evermore give us this bread."

"Forgive us our trespasses as we forgive those who trespass against us." To forgive is to love. You cannot make any spiritual progress in life except you practice the art of forgiveness. Supposing someone said something unkind or critical about you, suppose they smeared your character and you are smarting within from the hurt, forgive at once this way. Realize first of all that no one can really hurt you without your mental consent. You had to move in thought and feeling towards the other. The disturbance was created by yourself. If someone called you a skunk, are you a skunk? Of course not! How could it hurt you? You forgive the other by saying, "God's peace fills his soul." Undoubtedly he is mentally disturbed. Therefore, bless him and walk on in the Light.

You would not condemn a person who was a hunchback or who had Tuberculosis. Likewise, you must not condemn someone who is a mental hunchback, whose mind is twisted, distorted and under the sway of an evil or negative emotion. Have compassion on him and see God there and pray for his peace. You forgive the other when in your inmost thought and feeling you grant to the other person his Divine right to harmony, health, peace and all things good. You must always remember that there can be no real spiritual advance for you except when you sincerely claim for everyone on the face of the earth what you claim for yourself.

If you are resentful, angry or jealous of another, you are actually withholding and depriving yourself of harmony, health and peace. Remember the suggestion we give to another, we give to ourselves. If you try to interfere with the good fortune of another, you are at that moment depriving yourself of good for then you are trespassing on the rights of others. If, for example, you try to prevent the promotion of a fellow employee by lying about him or passing derogatory remarks to his superior, you are actually in a mood of lack and limitation and will attract loss in some way. Forgive yourself immediately by getting mentally absorbed with your aim or goal in life and at the same time identify yourself with the God in the other and rejoice in his spiritual, mental and material advancement. Forgive yourself whenever you find yourself prone to criticize, condemn or injure another. Substitute the negative thought with a Godlike thought. In other words, change your thought and keep it changed.

Having finished in South Africa I flew from Johannesburg to Perth, Western Australia, a distance of eight thousand miles, stopping at Mauritius Island and Coco Island. The latter island is small and beautiful. An Englishman got a coconut for me and showed how to break it open and suck the juice from it. It is a delicious food. I learned from him that the reason the island was never flooded or submerged even though it was the same level as the sea was, as he said, because of a Higher Wisdom which caused the coral insects to build a protective wall around the island, making sure nothing would happen to the island or its inhabitants.

Here you see an Infinite Intelligence at work forever watching over man and His creation.

The variegated colors of the sea surrounding the island is a scene of beauty and a joy forever. Australia is called the "sunshine continent." It is an open, smiling, beautiful land of trees, beaches, and vast ranches.

Perth is cosmopolitan and hospitable. Here Dr. Charles Randall conducts a very fine Truth Centre. He has been teaching Truth here for twenty years and is beloved by everyone. The students here are most devoted, loyal and wonderful. His work is progressing by leaps and bounds. I found a fresh interest in Truth in Perth by people in all walks of life. The Seekers Center, conducted by Mr. and Mrs. Webb is also a great blessing to Perth and the students are wonderful.

Dr. Randall had been wishing and praying that some teacher from America would visit him and tell him about our work in the U. S. A. I was happy to hear him and his people say that I answered that prayer. Dr. Randall told me of the remarkable healings through his consciousness of Divine Love and God's Presence. Here we had a marvelous spiritual feast.

Sydney is another wonderful city and the people are very progressive. Several business men told me that they were adapting American ideas to all business methods. The same applies in the engineering field. The executives I spoke to in Sydney make frequent trips to America to learn the latest methods in the field of art, science, industry and medicine. In a century the Australians have made a garden of Eden out of a wilderness.

Mrs. Grace Aguilar and her husband conduct the New Thought Movement in Sydney. They are most gracious and kind and have labored long in the vineyard. I spent eight days here, lecturing afternoons, and evenings and I enjoyed it immensely, meeting most interesting people. One leading business man in Sydney told me how, through prayer, he built his business and amassed a fortune blessing many. His constant prayer was, "God show me the way to give greater service to humanity." That was his only prayer. The Wisdom responded and he is being blessed in countless ways.

I am writing this chapter in Perth, Western Australia. I have just finished talking to a young woman who suffered for years from migraine headaches, sinusitis, stomach trouble and severe asthmatic attacks. She told me a sordid tale of bitterness, hostility, and hatred towards her mother. I asked her where her mother was and she said, "Oh, she's dead ten years." It seems the mother left the estate to her sister in New Zealand and all this time she was poisoning herself with that mental poison called hate. It is a real "killer." I explained to her what "forgive those who trespass against us" meant. Jesus said, "Forgive until seventy times seven," meaning one thousand times a day, if necessary.

She began to see that her mother acted according to her lights. Her mother did what she felt was right according to her state of consciousness, and that it was necessary for her to pray for her mother thereby blessing herself and her mother.

Prayer always prospers. Prayer heals the wounds of the heart. It stops the mouths of lions. It sets armies to flight. It opens prison doors. It turns water into wine and binds up the wounds of the brokenhearted. She wept copiously, which was good. It was a release and she said, "God bless my mother and His love be with her wherever she is." This was the healing balm necessary; this was the spirit of God speaking; it was the spirit of forgiveness, goodwill and understanding.

We prayed together for her mother, realizing that her mother was surrounded by God's Light, Love and Truth, that she was illumined and inspired and that God's Peace and Beauty filled her soul. God's Love welled up in her heart, and this was the benediction which healed this woman.

I never saw such a change in my life. A light came into this girl's eyes, a smile appeared on her countenance, a radiance seemed to surround and envelop her and she seemed suffused in the radiance of the Light Limitless. All symptoms vanished. She shouted out loud, "God is Love and I am healed!" She experienced in one moment the ecstasy of God's Love sometimes called "the moment which lasts forever."

Forgive until seventy times seven. Let us give ourselves the mood of love, goodwill, and understanding for our trespasses against the other. The cause of the girl's troubles were, of course, hatred, guilt complex and fear. She knew it was wrong to hate, this caused a guilt complex plus a fear of being punished for harboring the ill will.

Fear contracts the delicate mucous membranes which symbolize the envelope of God's Love, and when she entered into the spirit of forgiveness and filled her soul with love, she had an instantaneous healing.

Love frees, it gives, it is the Spirit of God. It is the Universal Solvent. It has neither height nor depth;

it neither comes nor goes. It fills all space and the ancients called it Love. You always know when you have forgiven the other. This is the acid test. Suppose someone told you some wonderful news about the person you say wronged you. How do you react? Do you resent it? Do you become disturbed? Would you rather hear the opposite? If so, you have not forgiven. The roots are still there. You wither the roots through prayer and love in the manner outlined and continue to do it until you are capable of rejoicing at hearing good news about the person who wronged you. You should rejoice to see the Law of God work for anybody regardless of who he is, what he is or where he is.

A Truth student in Sydney, Australia, where I gave a series of special public and class lessons, told me how he forgave another man who he said trespassed against him. You will find this interesting. He said, "I read your book review of 'Active Mind' by Orage in the New Thought Magazine where you said "Orage give you a wonderful treatment for solving your personal problems as follows: 'Compose a letter, written as from your friend to yourself, which would completely satisfy you if you received it. Put into it such words as you would like your friend to write or say to you.'" Then he added, "Your comment on that statement which was, 'This is the Law of Forgiveness,' impressed me immensely, and I applied it according to the statement in the book review." He added that he had been smarting from a letter received from his general manager and his attitude was, "This is the last straw—this I can't take." And he was boiling and seething with resentment, saying to himself, "This I can't forgive after all my years of faithful service, etc."

The Light came to this man as he read the book review and he sat humbly down and imagined the general manager had written him a letter which praised him and his work and which satisfied him in every way according to the Golden Rule and the Law of Love and Goodwill. He saw the words in the imaginary letter. He rejoiced in reading them and as he said to me, "I kept it up every night. I would read that letter over and over again and look at the general manager's signature." And all hatred left him as he continued to do this, and to quote him again, "The queerest thing in all the world happened!" The general manager wrote him a letter praising and promoting him, and the letter was the essence of what he had been imagining and feeling for several days. Here is shown the great law of substitution of forgiving, giving for, substituting the mood of Love and Goodwill for any feeling of ill will or hostility.

What this man did, anyone can do. All he did was to follow out instructions given in that article by imagining he had received the kind of letter he wanted in his heart to receive. As he lived that event in his mind and rejoiced in reading the contents of the imaginary letter, the all wise deeper self cast the spell of God around the general manager, causing him to respond in kind. You give love and you receive love. "Forgive and you shall be forgiven." LUKE 6:37. I said to this Truth student that actually no one can trespass against us without our mental consent. Consciousness is the only power and his state of consciousness, i.e., his habitual thinking, feelings, beliefs and opinions determined all his experiences, good or bad. He realized that the actions of others towards him reflected his inner mental attitude. They were simply instruments of the law which he had invoked, reminding him of his state of consciousness. Others are really messengers, telling us who we have conceived ourselves to be, and reminding us of the contents of our mentality. This man in Sydney had attracted that letter. Furthermore, as he told me, for many months he had deeply resented the fact that the general manager had not promoted him and yet had advanced others who were rather new with the organization. He felt that the general manager was very unjust, and unfair. The Light came to his mind, reminding him that the only thing wrong was his attitude, and his superior simply was testifying to his state of consciousness. His mind was full of recriminations and criticism and the intensity of this feeling caused the general manager's behavior toward him. When he mentally reversed his attitude and began to imagine and feel that he had heard what he longed and desired to hear, he was then uniting mentally with his aim, goal and desire in life and forgiving himself as well as the other. When the manager wrote him the letter he longed to receive, it was simply reflecting his changed mental attitude.

Begin now to cast the spell of God around you. You do this by entering into the feeling of the Spirit of Forgiveness, Love and Goodwill towards all. You are then surrounded by the spell of Goodwill, Truth and Beauty, and the envelope of His love surrounds you, enfolds you and enwraps you. Actually you are God intoxicated, and this mood of yours casts an enchanting spell on the minds and hearts of all those around you, causing them to think that their kindness, cooperation and goodwill towards you originate within themselves.

Orage in "Active Mind" under the chapter of "Dying Daily" suggests a pictorial review of all events of the day as you retire. Yes, you certainly could die mentally to all negative experiences by running a motion picture in your mind, mentally sensing, seeing and feeling a revised pictorial review of all experiences, conditions and events based on the Golden Rule and the Law of Love, which is the Spirit of forgiveness, understanding and goodwill. You will then die to all negativity and resurrect the qualities of god within you. Let us always remember the truth of the statement. "A man's foes are those of his own household." MATTHEW 10:36.

The Bible says, "Whosoever shall smite thee on the right cheek, turn to him the other also." The right cheek means your objective world, your body, environment, circumstances or conditions. If you find things unpleasant and others placing obstacles in your way, don't resent, hate or resist the evil condition mentally. "Turning the other cheek" means mental non-resistance which is superb mental strategy. In other words, if you resist evil you are giving it your attention, thereby magnifying it and perpetuating the condition. "Turn to him the other also." Quietly turn away mentally from the negative condition and place all your attention on what you want. Contemplate things as they ought to be. Begin to see God in the other. Identify yourself mentally with the God Presence and contemplate the Divine solution. Imagine things as they ought to be and feast on the reality that it is so. Stoutly maintain a confident attitude regardless of conditions. Refuse to yield or succumb to the feeling of despondency or gloom.

You turn the other cheek by giving yourself something for the negative thought. Detach your consciousness now from all unlovely and negative ideas and concentrate your attention on the ideal you wish to achieve. Your speech, your mannerisms, your eyes and general posture will denote whether you have for-given others and yourself. If you have truly forgiven the other, you will notify your face, your eyes and your speech. Have you notified your face and all your organs that you have forgiven everyone? If so, a heal-ing will follow.

There is a magnificent and wonderful movement in Japan called Seicho-No-Ie, meaning, "The Home of Infinite Life." It is the New Thought movement in Japan headed by that saintly and illumined soul Dr. Masahura Taniguchi. I spoke to his audience there. About two thousand were present at each lec-ture. They have one and a half million students of New Thought in Japan. Books are printed in English and Japanese; also, classes are given in English for Japanese-Americans as well as their own tongue. In one of his writings, Dr. Taniguchi cites several cases showing the power of forgiveness, i.e., giving yourself a new concept of life for the old materialistic concept.

In volume 4, number 3 of "Infinite Life, Wis-dom and Abundance" he states that during a severe flood in one of the provinces several restaurants were washed away in a certain town without leaving any trace behind; however, the restaurant Hiragi-ya, at

Yase, a meeting place for Japanese Truth students, was left intact. This was due to the mental attitude of the students who firmly believed that no calamity of any nature could ever befall them or their possessions. Dr. Taniguchi teaches his students that regardless of the natural calamity, if the student's mind is turned toward the Light, he will never be destroyed by the catastrophe.

In the book, just mentioned, Dr. Taniguchi refers again and again to men in Japan who were saved from train wreck, floods, earthquakes, ship disasters, etc. One striking instance was the case of one of his students who drove to a certain city in order to be on time for the boarding of a certain ship only to discover that he had been misinformed by a clerk regarding the sailing time. When he arrived, it had sailed about twenty minutes previously. He was indignant at the booking-clerk for giving him the wrong information. The ship he was to have sailed on met disaster due to collision. The article says the young man realized he was saved because he had the "Truth of Life" and he thanked God.

Practice the art of forgiving—giving for. Substitute for the belief in accident, misfortune, the concept of good fortune, security, peace of mind and an abiding faith in an Overshadowing Presence which watches over you by day and by night. Realize regularly and systematically that you and your possessions and all that is yours rest in the secret vault of the Most High, watched over and cared for by the wisdom of the Almighty and you will find that all your ways are ways of pleasantness, and all thy paths are peace. PROVERBS 3:17.

I quote from this Japanese pamphlet mentioned herein, "Even natural calamity cannot approach a person whose mind is illumined by the Light. Even if it approaches it cannot injure that person. Thunder, lightning, hail, and rainstorm will disappear when one prays knowing the Power of God. Heavy rain, windstorm, and earthquakes are all productions of the mind." Don't blame the weather conditions or the elements by stating that they are unfriendly, but simply forgive yourself. Cease blaming others for their trespasses against you. Realize that all that is necessary is the great art and science of prayer, which is the art of forgiving, giving yourself the Truths of God for the false theories, dogmas and concepts of life which have held you in thralldom and misery for years. Practice the art of forgiveness and thereby experience, "the Kingdom of God is at hand."

During a special class in Capetown held at the Science of Mind Center a brilliant lawyer, listening to a lecture on my recently published book "Believe in Yourself," gave me a clipping from a newspaper called

Argus, dealing with forgiveness. I quote a few pertinent paragraphs. "Lieutenant Colonel J. P. Carne told of his life as a prisoner in Korea. During his eighteen months solitary confinement he did not have a bitter word for the action of his Chinese captors in imposing a sentence so harsh that doctors were amazed at his survival. When walking around his garden (in England) listening to the church bells welcoming him home, Lieutenant Colonel Carne said, 'The mental picture of this glorious place (his loved ones, his garden, his home) forever kept my mind alive. Not for one moment did I let it slip from my memory. As I walked round and round that dusty Korean prison compound, devoid of all vegetation, I imagined in it every plant and tree in my garden and orchard. I saw them spring through the ground, grow and bloom. It was a vision I never let slip away.'" The caption of the article was "A Garden Gave Him Courage."

The above is a beautiful lesson in the art of forgiving. Instead of resenting, hating, or indulging in mental recriminations, he gave himself a new vision. He imagined himself at home with his loved ones; he felt the thrill and joy of it all; he imagined his garden in full bloom; he saw the plants grow and bring forth fruit. It was all vivid and real. He felt all this inwardly in his imagination, the great workshop of God (read "Believe in yourself "). Here is a quotation from Colonel Carne in the same article, "Never forget your home or your loved ones, is the only way to face such an experience." He said other men would have gone insane or perhaps died of a broken heart, but he saved himself because he had a vision. "It was a vision I never let slip away." His great secret in the art of forgiving was his faithfulness to his mental picture. He was loyal and devoted to his mental picture and never deviated from it by destructive inner talking and negative mental imagery.

Notice the inner speech of the above-mentioned Colonel. Never once did he become antagonistic, hostile, or bitter in his heart. His heart agreed with his lips. The inner movement of his heart agreed with his conscious mental movie; finally, both became one. The two agreed as touching on something, and it came to pass. This is what Ouspensky meant when he spoke of inner speech agreeing with your aim, purpose, plan or the Truth. Your aim is your goal, your objective, your plan, purpose, desire. Your thought and feeling is your word—does it agree with your desire or aim? In the book of Isaiah, it says, "My word shall not return unto me void, but it shall accomplish that which I please, and it shall prosper in the thing where-to I sent it." *Isaiah* 55:11.

Your word is really your inner feeling, your mood, tone or conviction. It is sometimes called the still small voice. You may not hear it with the ear, but it is something you sense. Your word of forgiveness must not be of the lips. It must be of the heart. Look upon your word as the movement of the spirit. Therefore, when you say, I have forgiven Mary or John, note that the forgiveness must be of the heart and not of the lips. The lips and the heart must agree, then God speaks, for the two have agreed and it is done. "If two of you shall agree on earth as touching anything that they shall ask, it shall be done for them of my Father which is in heaven." MATTHEW 18:19.

"In the beginning was the word." JOHN 1:1. The word of God is the idea, the formulated desire, the clear-cut concept. It is actually God defining Himself to be this, that or the other. Everything you see in the Universe is the word (idea, mould, image) of God made manifest.

A priest in one of the Buddhist temples told me to visit a Zen Buddhist monastery where tourists never go and which is rarely heard of. It is in the province of Fukie. There they pray and meditate in the silence. It is something you see and feel. It is an experience of the soul. It is something you never forget. The monks speak to each other without using words, or any outward sign of communication. Their thoughts are really their words. Their word is the inner sound or feeling of their heart. It is really a spiritual word. I could feel their greeting, their prayers. I could almost hear the unuttered sound. I conversed in the silence with them and understood their silent speech.

I was given food in the silence. I knew that they knew I was coming and a room was prepared and I remained over night and joined them in prayer and silent contemplation. When the words you speak audibly agree with the silent movements of your heart, agreement is reached. This is spiritual speech. Your prayer is answered. Forgiveness is no longer of the lips, it is now of the heart. Remember, the spoken word may not always agree with your inner feeling, and then, of course, nothing happens because it is the inner feeling that manifests itself.

Here I am in New Zealand, a country of wonderful scenery. The Southern Alps and its fiords the fertile and lush bushland, the beautiful lakes and magnificent waterfalls equal anything you might see anywhere. As in Australia you see thousands of sheep everywhere you go. The leader, Mr. Silcock of New Thought here, is a prominent business man and head of a large furniture company, supplying most exclusive furniture everywhere in New Zealand. He told me how he found his beautiful home by the lake. He simply read the 23rd Psalm and said to himself, "Our home is surrounded by green pastures and still waters." Here you see a beautiful, calm expanse of water, beautiful green country and thousands of sheep grazing. It is really a scene from the 23rd Psalm. Mr. and Mrs. Silcock were Divinely guided to this lovely spot showing you that you can use the wisdom of the Psalms for many purposes. The Bible contains the congealed wisdom of the ages and more and more wisdom can be extracted from it by meditation and prayer. Here Mr. Silcock plans and spends much time writing and meditating.

One of his students took me to see the thermal region of New Zealand and the Maori villages. The thermal region is fascinating. People live right in the area of these spouting geysers and smoke and are not the least bit afraid of an earthquake, though earthquakes have shook the area previously. The visitor gets a lesson in Truth by visiting the Waitomo caves, which are an underground fairyland of unbelievable beauty. The "glow worm grotto" is one of the most beautiful sights in New Zealand, where the boat which carries you through is guided by millions of tiny lights glittering in the dark cave. The guide gives a highly technical and involved explanation as to why the worms shine like stars, but as the Truth student with me said, "Why didn't he say 'Infinite Intelligence operating through the glowworm causes it to glow so that its light attracts small insects upon which they live.'" These glowworms also secrete a sticky, thready, fibrous substance, looking like long threads which trap the insects attracted by the light. This is the way the glowworm eats.

Here again we see a wisdom beyond the ken of man at work. In one of the caverns the guide tells you this cave is called the Cathedral and it certainly looks like one. Water, over a period of thousands of years seeping through the ground, acting on calcareous and other deposits, form exquisitely beautiful forms resembling statues, angels, churches and other marble edifices, showing again beauty, order, wisdom, symmetry and proportion inherent in the various chemical interactions of the substances forming these fairyland caves.

The New Thought people here have their own beautiful temple and organ. I enjoyed lecturing here very much, and I know that the work here grows, prospers and unfolds in a wonderful way.

A student in New Zealand asked me about "The Art of Forgiving." He said to me, "I don't know whether I have forgiven my brother or not; could you tell me?" He spoke about the will which his father left to his brother and, it was easy to detect he was still festering within. Yes, with words of the mouth he had been saying, "I forgive him." But it was not of the heart. He was still seething within. He was angry and upset about many things. Actually, he was centerless, confused, and as he said himself, "I know I am a neurotic!"

He was living in a shadow world of inner turmoil, strain, stress, full of resentment toward a brother who received all the father's estate twenty years previously. He learned that in order to truly forgive he must have a sincere, earnest desire to do so. He began to pray sincerely for his brother from the depths of his heart, wishing for him God's peace, love, abundance, and all good things. Every time he thought of his brother or when the memory of what he termed "the wrong" came to his mind, he watched his inner speech—his inner realm of feeling and immediately cremated and burned up the negative thought with the fire and love of the right thought, such as, "God is with him now; peace fills his soul; God and His love fills my mind." These and a dozen other spiritual concepts filled his mind whenever negative thoughts came. In the course of a few days he was completely at peace and went to see his brother and when they met they embraced. His stiff neck which had bothered him for many years was made whole immediately, He asked me to write it up in this book in the sincere belief it might help others. He forgave himself also by identifying himself with whatsoever things are true, lovely and of good report. The inner movement of his heart which represents his inner word began to pour Light and Truth on his brother and also on himself. His lips and heart agreed as touching upon Love, Peace, and Goodwill.

"The word is very nigh unto thee, in thy mouth, and in thy heart, that thou mayest do it. See, I have set before thee this day life and good, and death and evil." DEUTERONOMY 30:14, 15. "Choose ye this day whom ye will serve." JOSHUA 24:15.

What kind of thoughts have you chosen to meditate on? What are you giving attention to as you read these lines? Feast on peace, joy, gentleness, goodness, goodwill and understanding. Fill your mind with these concepts and then you are choosing life. Identify yourself with your desire for health, peace and prosperity. Bring your mind to think along these lines. Force yourself to think constructively, harmoniously and peacefully. Keep up the discipline and as you continue to remain faithful, you will begin to experience Life, something supremely worth experiencing—a life of peace, joy, happiness and security.

Always remember, it is the movement of your heart which gives validity to your word. What this student in Auckland was saying with his lips contradicted this inner feeling. It was the latter which was made manifest in his life as a stiff neck, confused neurotic mind, insomnia, etc. He decided to "choose life." Whatever you experience in your daily intercourse with people, always represents the outer picturing of your inner feeling and convictions.

People are always saying, "Oh, I have forgiven Mary. I have forgotten all about it." No, they haven't, for to forgive is to forget. They are still talking about the old grievance, still nourishing it with attention and each time they talk about it, they reinfect themselves.

Pray sincerely and honestly. Work with your mind regularly until you have established the conviction of good and your inner feeling will certainly be objectified.

"O God, the fabulous wings unused folded in the heart," Christopher Fry.

You have wings enabling you to soar aloft into the haven of God's peace and power. The wings are your thought and feeling. That is why a bird has two wings and that is why you have two wings. Regardless of what the difficulty is you don't have to fight it, quarrel or wage war or make a frontal assault. You can rise above it mentally and contemplate the Divine solution—the way it is in God and Heaven. The paradise of God is the mind at peace. God's paradise is within you. You can find it by stilling the wheels of your mind and think of God and realize the Infinite lies stretched in smiling repose within you.

This is the citadel of the Most High. Here you live beyond time and space. Here is the impregnable fortress, No one can lay siege to this citadel. That is where your wings take you. Here, fabulous wings are unused by millions. Feel the meaning of these words. You do this by writing them in your inward parts and inscribing them in your heart. To perceive these truths intellectually is one thing; to feel the truth of these beautiful words is another. Stop blaming others. There is no one to blame but yourself. Also, cease holding grudges, animosities or prejudices towards people. These are the chains and rivets which bind you to the wheel of pain. Loose them and let them go; release all the prisoners out of the prison of your mind. The greatest prison in the world is the mind of man full of fear, hatred, and ill will. "Stone walls do not a prison make nor iron bars a cage."

You don't have to go forth seeking peace, happiness, health, joy, or abundance. Why say, "Some day I will be happy. Some day I will have my health back. Some day I will be prosperous." God is the eternal now. Love is of God, eternal, indestructible. It has nothing to do with time or space. Peace is—it's of God. Why postpone peace? Claim it now, and the God of peace shall be yours. Choose happiness now by dwelling on whatsoever things are true, whatsoever things are just, whatsoever things are lovely, whatsoever things are pure. If there be any virtue, if there be any praise, think on these things.

"A man is what he thinks all day long." Emerson.

Engage your mind on the above God-given truths and you will experience happiness now. Why wait? To resent, to refuse to forgive, is to postpone health, joy, peace, etc. "The Kingdom of God is within you." Luke 17:21.

You don't have to go searching for God's qualities, attributes, and potencies. You don't have to go searching for your brain, do you? It's within you. You have been searching, yearning, longing, hoping, wishing, dreaming, yet all the while God and all His Glory was within you, and you had the "fabulous wings" unused, folded in your heart. Rise with your wings of faith and love and God shall give you Light. "Awake thou that sleepest, and arise from the dead, and Christ shall give thee light." Ephesians 5:14.

"Lead us not into temptation but deliver us from evil."

"Blessed is the man that endureth temptation: for when he is tried, he shall receive the crown of life, which the Lord hath promised to them that love him. Let no man say when he is tempted, I am tempted of God: for God cannot be tempted with evil, neither tempteth he any man: But every man is tempted, when he is drawn away of his own lust, and enticed." James 1:12–14.

Many people are under the erroneous belief that God is testing them or tempting them. I think it wise that they consider the 13th verse of the first chapter of James, and I am sure a complete healing of that false belief will follow. "Let no man say when he is tempted, I am tempted of God." The statement in the Lord's prayer, "Lead us not into temptation," deals with the function and the processes of man's mind. Here in this quotation you are told to be faithful to your announced plan and not deviate from your goal.

When you pray, you are endeavoring to unite mentally and emotionally with your ideal or goal. For example, talking here in Osaka, Japan to a prominent merchant, I found him full of fear because, as he said to me in perfect English, "The fortune teller told me the next three months would result in great business failure for me." He was enticed and drawn away from his announced goal, success and prosperity for himself, his organization and employees. "But every man is tempted when he is drawn away of his own lust, and enticed." JAMES 1:14. Instead of remaining faithful to the idea of success, he was now thinking of failure and filling his mind with thoughts of bankruptcy, the closing down of the store, no bank balance. You can see how his morbid imagination was operating. Actually he was envisaging a motion picture of his own creation in his mind. There was no reality behind it. As a matter of fact, he said to me, "Business is good," but then he added, "It can't last and it won't." I explained to him that success and failure were simply two ideas in the mind. If he meditated on failure, he would, of course, attract failure. If he imagined himself success-ful and began to feel that he was born to succeed, he would, of course, succeed.

To mentally unite with the idea of success and to know that you are then invoking a subjective power which responds to your habitual thinking is to create success. He began to see that the thing he was fear-ing did not exist save in his own mind. Furthermore, he began to see how he was seduced, enticed and carried away mentally by a false hypnotic suggestion which caused him to become gloomy, despondent and dejected. I spent an hour with him in his home. Before I left he realized success was of the mind and that he molded and fashioned and shaped his own destiny by his thought and feeling.

You can easily see how he was being tempted or caused to turn away from his goal by a suggestion of failure given to him by another. The fortune teller had no power and could not have exerted any influ-ence over this merchant except through his mental consent. He had to accept the suggestion of fear. He could have completely rejected the suggestion of lack and identified himself with the idea of suc-cess. In that way the false suggestion would have no effect.

"A man's foes shall be they of his own household." MATTHEW 10:36. The household is your state of mind and your victory over your enemy (negative thought) is to imagine and feel you now are what you want to be and remain faithful to your goal and according to your faith (mental attitude) is it done unto you. When you pray you must refuse to be seduced or tempted to yield to the thoughts of fear, lack, temptation. Do not give mental attention to doubt, anxiety, worry, for if you do, you are being tempted, i.e., you have permitted your mind to wander and unite with negativity and you fail to receive an answer to your prayer.

Here in India you meet people from all parts of the world. This is my second visit to this great and mysterious country. Some people call it the land of religions. I met people on the way to the Himalayas, and one Englishman was on his way to Tibet to visit the monasteries there. It is a colorful, interesting and fascinating country, full of fabulous temples, magnificent beautiful mosques, exotic bazaars. I met many people here who just came to see the Vale of Kashmir as well as some old friends.

I gave some talks in Calcutta and then visited a holy man with whom I have been corresponding for some time. I met him about thirty-three years ago in India. We chatted in the Lord Cecil Hotel, New Delhi, for a long time and then went to his retreat.

He had the wonderful capacity to talk to you silently. I could hear his thoughts though he was two rooms away from me. His thoughts became audible to me inside my ear and occasionally I conversed with him through thought in his retreat. We meditated together in his garden retreat and we were lifted up into fathomless dimensions of our Father's house. He told me he was going on to higher Dimensions, that he knew the day and hour and that it was near at hand. He said it is a greater work and he felt he could do much more. What he meant to convey was that he intuitively perceived when he was going on to the fourth Dimension. Several teachers whom I have known intimately have told me when they were going on. They were subjectively aware and they went on in their sleep. One of my teachers said to the students, "I am going to sleep at 2:00 p.m. Goodby." It was 10:00 a.m. and at 2:00 p.m. the leader passed on. My friend's comment to me was, "We all have to go some time and we have to go some way, in some manner. Our body had a beginning and, of course, it has an end, but we have bodies to infinity. There are celestial as well as terrestrial bodies."

On my way to Japan I heard of my friend's passing on—not by radio or telephone or letter, but he spoke clearly to me one thousand miles or more away, saying, "I'm going on now. Goodby. I sent you a letter a half hour ago." I received the letter and also one from his friend and it was exactly at that hour he passed on. He said he had passed on because his soul's work was finished on this plane. There is no death. Death is in our thought, not in the person we pronounce dead. My friend went on to open new doors in the House of Many Mansions.

Another great teacher, Emmet Fox, said in his writings, "I am going to live forever. A thousand years from now I shall still be alive and active somewhere, in one hundred thousand years still alive and active somewhere else."

I believe it would be a wonderful thing if we trained teachers for the foreign field. There is a tremendous opportunity in India and all over the world for the spreading of the New Thought message of Wisdom, Truth and Beauty. One of my traveling companions was all upset and boiling within because, as he said, he saw people fall in the street from apparent hunger and exhaustion and people passed them by, taking no notice of them. His anger is not the answer. His resentment does not help. When men see God's Truth and understand the laws of life, the milk of human kindness, compassion and goodwill will fill their souls. Knowledge of the spiritual principle which we teach and its application can and does heal the wounds of man.

Scientific prayer is the answer to the hunger of the world. It is the spiritual remedy for disease, war, hate and crime. Isaiah gives the answer, "The Spirit of the Lord God is upon me; because the Lord hath anointed me to preach good tidings unto the meek; he hath sent me to bind up the brokenhearted, to proclaim liberty to the captives, and the opening of the prison to them that are bound." ISAIAH 61:1.

The above is the answer to the world's problems. The day is fast approaching when people will bequeath vast sums of money and fortunes for mental and spiritual research to the Divine Science and Psychology movement and other similar organizations for the purpose of revealing to all men everywhere that the germs of cancer, TB, poliomyelitis, etc., will not be found in a test tube. The name of the germ is fear—it is in the mind of man.

I told an English woman in Calcutta, who asked me to refer to her case in this book without, of course, identifying her in any way, how to handle a difficult domestic problem. People told her that her husband was supporting an Indian woman and seeing her frequently. She said they were married for thirty-nine years and had a grown family. She was deeply resentful and hated this other woman like poison. She had permitted herself to be tempted or turned away from

God's love, peace, and goodwill. She had forgotten the spirit of forgiveness in her lust for revenge and to get even. She was ill. She was being led down a blind alley, not by God or any supposed Devil, for the only Devil in the world is the negative thoughts to which we yield or give attention. She didn't have to go along with the negative thoughts of resentment, hatred, and ill will. She had the power within her to completely reject such thoughts. Certainly they are unfit for mental consumption. She had the power to order the thoughts about, the same as you would order your store employees to attend to some business matter or routine. I explained to her how the captain on board the aircraft to Hong Kong showed me how they keep the aircraft on the beam. He showed me the beams of light and how they work and then pointed out how the ship was off the course fifteen miles due to bad weather, but in a matter of minutes it was right back on the beam and kept again traveling as God's plane through the heavens guided by His Light.

She saw that she was off the beam but the glory and wonder of it all is that she could instantaneously get back on the beam. "But this one thing I do, forgetting those things which are behind, and reaching forth unto those things which are before, I press toward the mark for the prize." Philippians 3:13–14.

She was drifting. She was off the beam of God's Glory, Light and Love. I told this woman she had to sincerely want to forgive and get back on the beam.

There must be a sincere hunger and thirst to do the right thing and then we are fifty-one percent over the hurdle and on the way to peace of mind. The Psalmist tells you about this true desire for inner transformation when he says, "As the hart panteth after the water brooks, so panteth my soul after thee, O God." PSALMS 42:1.

She came to the point. She made a decision and charted her spiritual course of action. The solution was simple. Prayer was the answer, and prayer is to accept the gift of God which is already given. "Every good gift and every perfect gift is from above, and cometh down from the Father of lights with whom is no variableness, neither shadow of turning." JAMES 1:17. "Let every man be swift to hear, slow to speak, slow to wrath." JAMES 1:19. Be swift in hearing the good news but never indulge in negative thinking or in the mood of anger. Go within at once and galvanize yourself into the feeling of being what you long to be.

Here is how the woman healed the situation. She decided on my instructions to bless her husband. When you bless someone you identify that person with God's qualities and attributes and remain faithful to the God in the person. Each person you meet is

an Incarnation of God and all you have to do is to realize what is true of God is true of the other. She prayed
and truly blessed her husband by frequently saying
with all the feeling and love at her command, "My
husband is God's man. What's true of God is true of
him. My husband is expressing God's love, harmony
and peace of mind. He is Divinely guided and illumined by the Light. There is only Divine Love, Divine
Peace and Harmony between us. I salute the Divinity
in him." When thoughts of fear, worry or resentment
came into her mind, she would immediately turn to
the Spiritual Truth about him and silently claim, "He
is God's man and God is being expressed through
him," and other similar statements. The point was
that she really meant it. She kept her eye on the beam
of God's Glory. She knew that he who perseveres to
the end shall find the answer. She was devoted, loyal,
and faithful to her announced goal which was Harmony and Love, where discord and confusion reigned
previously. Love is an emotional attachment and she
became attached mentally and emotionally to the
truths of God.

I told her that as she gave her attention to the truth
of God about her husband and persevered she would
ultimately build a state of consciousness which would
precipitate itself as experience into her life. Sooner or
later she would qualify her consciousness and reach

a climax of fulfillment and then the answer would come. Never once was she to permit her mind to wander after false Gods. To do so would rob her of her strength and faith and nullify her prayer.

Whole-souled devotion to the Truth is essential. You must not permit extraneous material such as fear, doubt, worry and other negative concepts to creep into your mentality. To do is to be seduced, is to be tempted, or caused to turn away from your true ideal and goal in life. You must be loyal to your chosen ideal or goal.

This woman was loyal to God and the Truth. She never once faltered. She was faithful all day long. She prayed without ceasing, which means she maintained the right mental attitude in spite of all appearances and unpleasant episodes and abusive treatment. She knew the Truth must win, and win she did. The third night the husband came home and said to her, "Here is the diamond bracelet I was taking to the other woman. You are the one I love." He asked forgiveness and admitted he was a fool, saying, "There is no fool like an old fool."

"Deliver us from evil." You deliver and free yourself from all negative experiences by realizing that you can have all things you want in life through the law of God. The law is, "I am that which I contemplate." Troward says it this way, "All things are made by the self-contemplation of spirit." I am that which I feel myself to be. Whatever you claim as true of yourself you become. The Power responds to your belief and to believe is to accept something as true. Then the Power responds accordingly and distributes itself in your world as health, wealth, abundance, etc. It is all done according to your belief. You don't have to hurt anyone in the world to get what you want. You can go to the same Eternal Fountain and drink of the water of Life. The price is belief, faith, conviction. All men can pay that price. States of consciousness manifest themselves. The Bible says, "Go in and possess the land," which means to go within your own consciousness and there claim and feel you now are what you long to be—that you possess what you long to possess and as you remain faithful to your claim and press your claim you will experience and manifest it.

Spell the word "evil" backward and you have your answer. It means to live life backward. You are here to learn to differentiate, to distinguish and choose between a good apple and a rotten apple, to eat the right berries and not the poison-out berries on the bush. You must learn when you are young not to play with snakes, but it is all right to play with dogs. Likewise, in the realm of the mind, you must refuse mental food unfit for mental and spiritual consumption. You must learn to reject all unsavory mental food. Follow the injunction of the Bible which states in majestic, spiritual overtones, "Get thee behind me, Satan: thou art an offence unto me: for thou savourest not the things that be of God, but those that be of men." MATTHEW 16:23.

All this means is that you are now awakening to the Truth and you positively and definitely refuse to indulge in vicious and destructive thinking. Satan means to err, to slip, to make a mistake It comes from the word Sata—to err. You err when you fail to contemplate God and all things God-like. You are here to separate the sheep from the goats while sitting on the Throne of your Glory. All of which means, your throne is your consciousness of authority, your spiritual awareness which enables you to reject everything false, foolish and superstitious and choose all things according to spiritual standards.

I have just finished talking to a very wonderful spiritual man here in Japan. He told me many interesting and fascinating experiences. Incidentally, I might mention, he is arranging for me an introduction to the Abbott of one of the oldest Zen Monasteries in Japan. I have wished to see the inner workings of this Temple and the answer came through him. You never know how the answer comes. In class I discussed some of these experiences. I rarely, if ever, go the way of tourists. They are shown what the people want them to see. You must go away from the beaten track and enter into the life and the home experience of people in foreign lands in order to know them and feel what goes on in their minds and hearts.

There are two thousand Truth Centres in Japan and eight thousand New Thought reading rooms. There are hundreds of voluntary teachers who travel from point to point. There are a great number of specially trained personnel who go from Tokyo to lecture, teach and heal. They have most remarkable healings.

A most interesting thing I just heard is that a great number of communist leaders who have been released from jail, and were considered tough, ruthless, and fanatical are now teaching New Thought openly and with greater zeal than they ever taught communism. Dr. Taniguchi, the founder of New Thought in Japan, says all they do is give them or send them literature and pray and the miracle happens. They follow the instruction: "Resist not evil, overcome evil with good."

I listened to Dr. Taniguchi, the world famous teacher of New Thought in Japan, interpret Buddhist scripture writings for his audience like I interpret the Old and New Testament every Sunday morning to my people. Dr. Taniguchi is a dedicated man, a great spiritual leader, and he went through many schools of thought and at last saw the Light—one God and the way He works. God is all, there is nothing else. Dr. Taniguchi has built the most beautiful New Thought Temple in all the world. It is magnificent. I spoke to overflow audiences in this temple.

Here in Hong Kong, which means fragrant harbour, so Chinese and yet so British, is a land of enchanting contrasts. In parts of the city the ways of thousands of years ago still persist, showing the power of traditional concepts and mental atmosphere. Children grow up in the image and likeness of the dominant mental atmosphere of the home. Hong Kong, on the whole, is a great modern city of fabulous, spectacular beauty. Here you see emerald hills and sapphire bays. Ships from all parts of the world stop here. In the lobby of the Peninsula Hotel, you will see people from all parts of the world. I must now tell you about a Chinaman I met.

I bought some material from him and I saw he was intensely worried, gave me wrong change twice and also wrong merchandise. I asked him what the trouble was, and he said, "You are a minister?" I said, "Yes." He said, "I knew you were the minute you walked in the door." His trouble was that he was afraid of being shot because, as he said, "I wouldn't go along with them in their nefarious scheme."

"Deliver us from evil." This is not a pious petition or supplication asking a Deity to keep evil away.

The Bible is teaching you correct mental and spiritual laws. I asked this Chinaman, "Can God be killed?" He said, "No, of course, not." "Well," I said, "that's all you have to think—God is the reality of you and God can't be slain. Keep your mind on that ideal." He had a Bible in his hand, an English Bible; he spoke excellent English. I opened it at JOHN 6:44. "No one can come to me, except the Father which hath sent me draw him." I explained to him the meaning of that passage which is simply this, that no manifestation or experience can come into your life except your own consciousness attracts it. I went on by saying that if he saw two men fighting and one pulled the trigger and shot the other, the man who was shot actually killed himself. That is the law. Many people can't see that. Nevertheless, it is the absolute Truth. Nothing happens to man except his own consciousness decrees it consciously or unconsciously. Both men were in a murderous mental attitude and the external killing was simply the manifestation of the man's internal destruction. The man who committed the murder, of course, is also responsible for his state of consciousness. He has killed Love, Peace, Goodwill, Harmony. He has killed his reason and his whole mentality is at war with himself. Fear and a guilt complex follows. He has slain the Peace of God in himself. He lives in fear of the electric chair and of the prison and of course, later on, policemen will come and put him in prison. But he placed himself in that prison thousands of times before it happened objectively. He is now suffering a psychological and spiritual death.

He seemed to follow this fairly well. I wrote a prayer for him somewhat like this, "There is only one Presence and one Power. I honor this Presence in my heart. There is no other. I now know no one in all the world can hurt me without my permission. I refuse to give mental consent or permission to anyone in the world to hurt me. I give no power to external conditions, to any person. I radiate God's Love, Peace and Harmony to all these men (mentioning their names). God is with them and acting through them. I am surrounded by the Love of God which is the invincible armor of God. It is wonderful. God is with me and all is well." I instructed him to pray this way fifteen minutes, three times daily. As he did so these truths would sink into his subconscious mind and he would be at peace.

I just received a most marvelous letter from him saying that he never felt better in his life and that all fear had left him. Then there is a postscript to the letter which read, "I saw by the evening paper they were all drowned at sea this morning." He was delivered from evil, negative imagery, and fear thoughts by prayer. The sequel or way the prayer is answered is always past finding out. "As the Heavens are above the earth so are My ways above your ways." There must have been a great fear of death on the part of the men who were drowned—again a state of consciousness. It is not an angry God drowning people or punishing people. States of consciousness always manifest themselves. When we destroy the enemy in our mind through faith and loyalty to the one True God we are at peace. When a person is drowned or when he meets with sudden death or is accidentally shot, the thing to remember is that you don't know the contents of the other person's consciousness. You haven't seen his habitual thinking, his moods, feelings and beliefs. His religion and environmental training plus his habitual mental atmosphere have entered into the conditioning of his consciousness. The race-mind believes in accidents, misfortunes, calamities, death and failure, etc. It must be clear to anyone who wants to think at all that if we do not consciously choose and direct our thought life, the world, or race mind will gradually impinge itself on our deeper mind and unconsciously we will attract negative experiences, not perhaps because we consciously gave our attention to these things, but rather that we failed to think spiritually and constructively.

This is why Jesus said, "Except ye repent ye shall likewise perish," meaning except we change our thought and keep it changed we too shall be victims of the race mind. We are all immersed in the great collective unconscious of which Carl Jung speaks. We are receiving the thoughts, feelings and beliefs of the world mind now according to the degree of our receptivity. We are giving and receiving all day long. You are a broadcasting station as well as a receiving station. Subjectively we are one with all men in the world. Quimby said, "Our minds mingle like the atmosphere and each has his identity in that atmosphere." The man who does not pray or direct his thinking is just one of the herd and is pushed around by every wind that blows. Ask your friend, "Did you get the flu this year?" She will answer, "No, not yet." She is expecting it, isn't she? The flu is a belief of the race mind.

Sickness is a race belief. If you don't believe in sickness and realized because God could not be sick, you couldn't—then, of course, you would never be sick, you couldn't be. If you really did not believe in a physical death, you would not leave any physical evidence of it. Fear is the death of faith. Hate is the death of love. Confusion and anger are the death of peace. Sorrow, grief and gloom are the death of joy. These are the thieves, robbers and murderers which rob, steal and kill our peace, happiness and health.

A man who had listened to one of the lectures visited me in the Hotel and said, "Why is it that I have done good all my life and yet evil follows me wherever I go, whatever I do?" He then proceeded to tell me all the good he had done and is doing for people and for the world, and it was very impressive. He gave large sums of money to the poor, to churches, and charitable organizations, he went regularly to church, sang hymns and did all the things he was supposed to do according to ritual and formula. He was really bitter toward God because, as he said to me, "God has let me down. I do his work and evil follows." He then cited misfortune after misfortune which had befallen him and his family in spite of all his good works. He said the wicked seem to prosper like the green bay tree. All this sounds rather convincing, but there was an obvious error in the whole story. I asked him a simple question when he had finished and it was this, "Tell me about your thought life—that's what I want to know, for that which we sow, we reap." What we are in the inner world of the mind is what we experience on the outside. His inner realm of thought and feeling was full of recriminations, bitterness and condemnations. He was angry toward God. His thoughts were erroneous and highly negative and naturally he evoked and called forth the automatic response of his own unconscious mind.

Think good, good follows. Think evil, evil follows. He was thinking more or less in a confused manner.

Nevertheless he was operating a law which responded according to the nature of his thought. A man may be kind to animals, give candy to babies and repeat some prayers by rote, not knowing what they mean, in a sort of perfunctory manner. He may pay his taxes and be nice to the neighbors. All this is good and it is as it should be, but in his inner life he also must practice goodness, truth and beauty. His thoughts, feelings and reactions to life must coincide with the Golden Rule, the Law of Love and the Spirit of Forgiveness.

"Whatsoever things are true, whatsoever things are honest, whatsoever things are just, whatsoever things are pure, whatsoever things are lovely, whatsoever things are of good report; if there be any virtue, and if there be any praise, think on these things." Philippians 4:8. This is the answer to the question. God's gifts were waiting for this man, but he had to open his mind to receive them. "Bring ye all the tithes into the storehouse, that there may be meat in mine house, and prove me now herewith, said the Lord of hosts, if I will not open you the windows of heaven, and pour you out a blessing, that there shall not be room enough to receive it." MALACHI 4:10.

I told this man all he had to do was to completely change his mental attitude and begin to completely accept in his mind that God's fullness was flowing through all the departments of his life, that he was

Divinely guided and blessed in all ways. He decided to cease all negative thinking and from that moment forward to assume that Divine guidance, prosperity and right action would come forth in his life in the same way as the sun comes forth in the morning.

To enter into the spirit and wonder of it all is to open the windows of heaven and receive the blessing which was always there. He began to feel inwardly that he was guided, blessed and prospered, and he began to accept it mentally and decided to live in that mental atmosphere, and as the clouds become saturated and fall as rain, so will his changed mental attitude result in mercy and love and fall as the gentle rain from heaven. I haven't heard from him, but I know from the Light in his eyes and the radiance of his smile that the windows of heaven are opened for him and as I write I am sure his mind is open to receive the dew of heaven.

It is our mission to ask wisely. We must learn how to pray aright. Our pains, aches and illnesses are life's response to our negative thinking, causing us to seek the Light and the cause. You are the creator of your own good and your negative experiences. Decide now to experience the glory and beauty of life. It is your mission and purpose in life to go up the Hill of God, expressing ever higher and higher states of consciousness, revealing to yourself and the world a grander and greater measure of His infinite wisdom, glory and power. Remember always that there is but One Power and One Presence. There is no other power to challenge, oppose or thwart the Infinite One. "There cannot be two infinites." Troward says, to repeat a quote, "If there were two opposing powers one would cancel out the other and there would be chaos instead of a cosmos." This power is your own awareness, your own consciousness, your own "I am" is God, the Infinite One, the very life of you. This is the mystery hidden from all generations. This is your foundation, the rock upon which you build your whole future. What is true of God is true of you.

To know and realize this is to become filled with a mystic awe, a reverence, a devotion which words cannot describe. You begin to realize what the poet meant when he said, "Closer is He than breathing, nearer is He than hands and feet." It is God believing himself to be you. You are God expressed for there is but One Being, One Life and all of us are the One Life made manifest. We couldn't be anything else for there is no other. "Hear, O Israel: The Lord our God is one Lord." DEUTERONOMY 6:4.

The evil that man is experiencing is due to his belief in another power. He is full of beliefs in secondary causes. Man must come back to the One, the Beautiful and the Good. It is written, "Hear, O Israel; The Lord our God is one Lord: And thou shalt love the Lord thy God with all thy heart, and with all thy soul, and with all thy mind, and with all thy strength: this is the first commandment. And the second is like, namely this, Thou shalt love thy neighbour as thyself. There is none other commandment greater than these." MARK 12:29–30–31.

"If a man say, I love God and hateth his brother, he is a liar; for he that loveth not his brother whom he hath seen, how can he love God whom he hath not seen? And this commandment have we from him, That he who loveth God love his brother also." EPISTLE JOHN 4:20–21. The evil which man experiences would begin to vanish if he gave all his allegiance and devotion to one supreme power, recognizing no other. There is, as the commandment tells you, only one Power, one God, one Love, one Life, one Father of all. The Fourth Epistle of John really tells you in plain language that if you truly worship the one power, you will likewise express that love, respect and goodwill to your brother man. "If a man say, I love God and hateth his brother, he is a liar." Love is an emotional attachment, complete loyalty and allegiance to ONE—the one God.

Put your heart and soul into applying the Truths of God into your life and as you establish peace in your own mind and when your heart is full of love and goodwill to all, you will find that an inner peace becomes real and actually you begin to love all men everywhere, wishing for them all good things. Your love is now a spirit of forgiveness, an understanding and a sincere blessing and goodwill to all. "He who loves God loves his brother also." Here really, is the way to a happy, healthy and prosperous life. Your intense passion and desire to transform yourself plus your faith in an everlasting Power which responds to your thought, sets the creative law in motion (action and reaction) and the result is bliss, peace, happiness and joy. You know whatever is true of God is true of you, and as you claim that God's qualities, attributes and potencies are yours, and as you continue to do so, the God Presence responds accordingly. Your desire, plus your faith unite in a mystic marriage of the soul, and the offspring of such a union is peace, health, and joy. You have triumphed over evil, pain and trouble. God and His love fills your soul, and where love is there is no evil. Loving God and the good, you are in love with all men. "And we have known and believed the love that God hath to us. God is love; and he that dwelleth in love, dwelleth in God, and God in him." Epistle of John 4:16.

3

My Visit To Honolulu

I am writing the last chapter of my book in this beautiful city of Honolulu, Hawaii. I was pleasantly surprised to be met at the Honolulu airport on my flight from Japan by about sixteen Japanese and they placed so many leis around my neck that my face couldn't be seen. The New Thought movement in Japan where I spoke cabled them, telling them I was coming and to invite me to speak. I enjoyed speaking at the New Thought Temple here called Seicho-no-le, meaning Infinite Life Movement. The building is spacious and beautiful and their leader and members of the Board are dedicated men. Speaking in their Temple in Honolulu was a great joy and a magnificent spiritual vibration permeated the entire atmosphere. The people here are going from glory to glory.

"For thine is the kingdom, and the power, and the glory, for ever. Amen." MATTHEW 6:13. Here the inspired writer enters into a paeon of exultation and praise about the God presence within. Here you are reminded in majestic cadences which whisper and murmur in your heartstrings that the Kingdom of God is within you. All the wisdom, power and intelligence of the Infinite One is within you, waiting for you to call upon it. "The Kingdom of God is at Hand." The Love, the Peace, the Health, the Joy, the Answer you are seeking—all these are within you. They are present from the foundation of time. Don't wait for peace. Peace is of God. Tune in on the Infinite One now and let His river of peace flood your mind, your heart, your whole being. You will then discover that truly the Kingdom of God and His peace IS at hand. It is here now. "The works were finished from the foundation of the world." HEBREWS 4:3. This is the whole story of prayer and religion.

The work being finished, all that you have to do now is to open your mind and heart and receive the gift of God. God is the giver and the gift. Man is the receiver. Begin now to contemplate the finished works of God and cease saying, "Someday I will be happy." Don't postpone the coming of God's Kingdom, of Peace, Harmony and Joy. "Wherefore I put thee in remembrance that thou stir up the gift of

God, which is in thee by the putting on of my hands."
TIMOTHY 1:6.

Change your thoughts and former concepts of an
evil, disordered, chaotic world and realize that all is
perfect in God and Heaven. In the midst of a storm
at sea, deep down in the ocean there is absolute calm.
The same is true of you and your world. Underneath
the fretting, fussing and fuming, behind all of man's
inhumanity to man there is an ever abiding peace,
an everlasting law of righteousness and an absolute
bliss and harmony. "I am God, and there is none like
me. Declaring the end from the beginning, and from
ancient times the things that are not yet done." ISAIAH
46:9-10. Here in simple, beautiful, Biblical language,
you are told that man creates nothing. He only gives
form and expression to that which is already created,
just the same way as Edison did not make electricity,
he released it or made it manifest in your home so that
you can use that which always was from the foundation of time.

Moses could have used television, radio or loud
speakers in his day. The principle and all things necessary for this manifestation always existed waiting
for him to use them. You don't create Love, Joy, Harmony, or Health. You express these qualities by reor-
ganizing your mental pattern according to harmony
and peace, and immediately you express these quali-

ties of God. Your sickness, pain and aches are due to disorganized thought patterns. Reorder your mental patterns and perceive the Truths of God which are eternal and change not and again you will experience that which you thought you had lost. Don't think for one minute you are going to become more spiritual next year or fifty years from now. Spiritual growth and expression has nothing to do with time and space. God and His attributes are timeless and spaceless. In the prayer process you leave time and space and you enter Eternity—timeless, spaceless, and formless and as you contemplate God and His love you become more Godlike every day. All that you ever hope to be, you are already. All that is necessary is to believe and assume you are it and you become it. It is here now. Don't say, "Some day I will be a great teacher." You are the teacher now, the All-Wise one is within you. I am sure you can't imagine God learning something, or that God is growing, expanding or evolving. God is and all there is is God.

The Book of Hebrews which I quoted from tells you that all the works are already finished. "I am the beginning and the end, there is nothing to come that has not been and is."

I like what an Indian sage in Ceylon said to me, "When I read your scripture I say, 'What did I mean when I wrote the book of John or what did I mean when I wrote Genesis?'" He said that he read the Vedas and Upanishads and all Sacred Literature the same way. This is a beautiful and a really wonderful way to read the Bible or Plato or any great works. Consciousness wrote all books, i.e., your real self, the self of every man. There is only One Being playing all roles. Therefore, when you awaken to this you realize you have been everywhere, you have seen everything, you have written everything. You have played all roles. You have been Jesus, Moses, Buddha, Mohammed, Plato and all men who ever lived.

There is only one Being dramatizing Himself as the many. This one Being is indivisible. It is now playing the role of the reader of this book. You have been everywhere; you have seen everything and the whole world and all of creation is within you. You (i.e., your consciousness) wrote all Bibles, spoke all languages. Your estimate and mental blue print of yourself determines what you are now experiencing. All tones are in the piano, but it depends how you play whether you strike a discord or play a melody of God. The principle of Harmony plus the tones and notes were there from the foundation of time. You can play "Pop Goes the Weasel" or a Beethoven Sonata. All that you desire now whether true place, a healing, inspiration, guidance, or prosperity already exists. All that is necessary is for you to believe that this is so.

Enter into the feeling of being or possessing what you long to be or possess and you will experience the manifestation, for according to your belief is it done unto you. Change your belief about God, Life and the Universe. Claim that all the things that are true of God are true of you and you will enter into the Kingdom, the Power and the Glory.

It is wonderful for you to contemplate that Omnipotence is within you. This is the power that moves the planets effortlessly and sustains the galaxies in space. This gives you a feeling of reverence and you begin to feel the truth of the statement, "With God all things are possible." Just imagine for a moment that all the atomic, nuclear and electric power of the world is as nothing compared to that which is ALL. The Glory is the Light of God. When the writer says, "Thine is the Glory," he is referring to the Infinite Intelligence of God which created all things, sustains all things and governs the entire cosmos. For example, the Living Intelligence made your body, created all its organs, cells, tissue and muscles. Your conscious and subconscious mind are projections of it. It is the same Intelligence which guides the planets in their course and causes the sun to shine. It is the Intelligence, or Light which watches over the birds. "Behold the birds of the air, they toil not, neither do they gather into barns, yet

God feedeth them." It is marvelous to contemplate the fact that God knows only the answer.

I was wondering last night what to say to a man from Persia who is staying where I am at present. So I went to sleep saying, "God, you know the answer for Thine is the Glory." I went off to sleep just dwelling mentally on the answer, nothing else. In the morning, I told him what was revealed to me and his reply was most significant. "Thank you, Brother, to God is the Glory." The glow and the ray (Glory) mean the warmth of His Love and the radiance of the Light Limitless.

In the class I gave on the Psalms at the Wilshire Ebell Theatre which was so immensely popular that I regularly receive letters saying, "When will you repeat the Psalms?" I gave the inner meaning of the 139th Psalm, one of the most beautiful, soul stirring and illuminating psalms in the whole Bible. Dr. Evans, the famous follower of Quimby, saw and understood its meaning. To him it was the key to all spiritual healing. It shed its glory on him. "My substance was not hid from thee, when I was made in secret, and curiously wrought in the lowest parts of the earth. Thine eyes did see my substance, yet being unperfect; and in thy book all my members were written, which in continuance were fashioned, when as yet there was none of them." PSALMS 139:15–16.

One young girl in the class meditated on what was said and when she went home, she began to talk to herself saying in effect, "The Living Intelligence which made and fashioned my body even before any of my organs appeared must have a pattern and a prototype of all organs, cells, tissues, etc. It must know how to remake a damaged organ inasmuch as it is the Creator and maker of the body." She heard the explanation about the little boy who was told that the man who made the Frigidaire could fix it and then the little boy was told God made his toe and could mend it too, if he asked him. The little boy, prior to sleep, said, "God, you made this toe; I want service on this toe. I want it now. Thank you. Amen." The little boy's toe was made whole. The Living Intelligence responded to the boy's belief and expectation. He expected service from the maker of his toe, like you would expect service from the maker of your ice box or washing machine. If it is out of order, the manufacturer knows what is wrong and certainly can adjust it. This is what the Psalmist is telling you. He says in effect, "In thy book all my members were written." The book is your deeper or subjective mind which created your body and all its organs. In that Book or Divine Mind is the perfect pattern or idea behind a heart, lung, liver, brain, or any organ. "All my members (organs) were written," which in continuance were fashioned, and came forth in regular order, gradually and systematically, so that in nine months the child is fully grown in the womb. "When as yet there was none of them." All your organs came out of the invisible. God's fully grown man was already in the cell, in the womb, in the same way as the fully grown oak tree is in the subjective mind even though you do not see it within the acorn. How could the acorn become the oak except the fully grown pattern already existed in the Divine Mind.

This young girl meditated on these truths and then she began to claim regularly and systematically, "The Living Intelligence which made my body now takes over and it is restoring, healing every atom of my being, making my whole body conform to God's perfect pattern of Harmony, Health and Peace." There was understanding and faith in that prayer. She knew what she was doing and why she was doing it. She turned her damaged or diseased organ over to its maker for service and she demanded service like the little boy demanded it for his toe. She had a wonderful healing through the appreciation of the wisdom of the Psalm.

Begin now to realize that God knows only the answer. Infinite Intelligence could not have a problem. It has the answer. The greatest desert in the world is not Arizona, Sahara, or Mojave, it is in the wilderness of man's mind which is full of miscellaneous growths of all kinds, such as fear, doubt, worry, ignorance, superstition as well as other sorts of sundry concepts of a foolish nature.

Realize once and for all time that the Kingdom of Heaven is within and that it is the Father's good pleasure to give you the Kingdom. "Son thou are ever with me, and all that I have is thine." LUKE 15:31. Prepare your mind to receive the good which already is. "Prepare ye the way of the Lord, make straight in the desert (your mind) a highway for our God." ISAIAH 40:3.

As you enthrone God in your mind by regularly claiming, "Infinite Intelligence leads and guides me in all my ways," you know that the premise established in your mind is true. Therefore, the automatic response of the deeper self will be in accordance with your request. In other words, the result will be right and good and true. Keep on doing this and "Every valley (depressed state) shall be exalted, and every mountain and hill (obstacles) shall be made low, and the crooked (difficulties, entanglements) shall be made straight, and the rough places plain." ISAIAH 40:4.

When you turn to the God Power realizing the Kingdom is within, know also that It answers you in Its own way. Simply trust It and believe It, like you trusted your mother when you were a child. You looked into her eyes and you saw Love there. Look to the Infinite Love and Goodness of God.

Love is Trust. Don't say How, When, Where or through what sources. Simply believe "For as the heavens are higher than the earth, so are my ways higher than your ways, and my thoughts than your thoughts." Isaiah 55:9. "For my thoughts are not your thoughts, neither are your ways my ways, saith the Lord." Isaiah 55:8.

It is wonderful to begin to practice trusting the Infinite Intelligence within you, to become a lamp unto your feet and a light on your path. Keep it up through habitual thinking and finally it becomes a dominant conviction. Then you have the real Lord or God Wisdom in charge of your mind as Ruler and Governor and then "Thy sun shall no more go down; neither shall thy moon give light unto thee: but the Lord shall be unto thee an everlasting light, and the days of thy mourning shall be ended." Isaiah 60:20.

Cease giving power to a world of effect. The only power is God—your own Consciousness. There is no other. Let spiritual thoughts and the mood of confidence and faith plus the conviction in all things good rule, govern and guide the Kingdom of your mind. Then you are singing the song of the jubilant soul who wrote in the Bible, "The sun shall be no more thy light by day; neither for brightness shall the moon give light unto thee; but the Lord shall be unto thee an everlasting light, and thy God thy Glory." Isaiah 60:19.

"For thine IS the Kingdom, the Power and the Glory forever and ever. Amen."

About the Author

A native of Ireland who resettled in America, Joseph Murphy, Ph.D., D.D. (1898–1981) was a prolific and widely admired New Thought minister and writer, best known for his metaphysical classic, *The Power of Your Subconscious Mind*, an international bestseller since it first appeared on the self-help scene in 1963. A popular speaker, Murphy lectured on both American coasts and in Europe, Asia, and South Africa. His many books and pamphlets on the auto-suggestive and metaphysical faculties of the human mind have entered multiple editions—some of the most poignant of which appear in this volume. Murphy is considered one of the pioneering voices of affirmative-thinking philosophy.

Printed in the USA
CPSIA information can be obtained
at www.ICGtesting.com
JSHW012040140824
68134JS00033B/3178